WASHINGTON
DISASTERS

DISASTERS SERIES

WASHINGTON
DISASTERS

TRUE STORIES OF
TRAGEDY AND SURVIVAL

Rob McNair-Huff
and Natalie McNair-Huff

Globe
Pequot

Guilford, Connecticut

Globe
Pequot

An imprint of Rowman & Littlefield

Distributed by NATIONAL BOOK NETWORK

Copyright © 2016 by Rowman & Littlefield

British Library Cataloguing in Publication Information Available

Library of Congress Cataloging-in-Publication Data Available

ISBN 978-1-4930-1322-7 (paperback)
ISBN 978-1-4930-1323-4 (e-book)

♾™ The paper used in this publication meets the minimum requirements of American National Standard for Information Sciences—Permanence of Paper for Printed Library Materials, ANSI/NISO Z39.48-1992.

Contents

Introduction

As a state that has been shaken by epic earthquakes, swept by lava and ice, and gradually settled as one of the last bastions of the Wild West, Washington's history is full of tales of disaster and narrow escape.

Washington is a state shaped by disaster. Floods of magma formed the Columbia River basin in eastern Washington, and near the end of the last Ice Age, glacial floods swept across that same river basin and created the scenic Columbia River Gorge. These two powerful natural events rank among the largest in world history. Even the sub duction zone earthquake that struck off the Washington coast in 1700—the first story in this book—ranks as one of the most powerful earthquakes in history.

Washington Disasters takes a look at twenty-two notable disasters in the short history of the state. Beginning with the Native American mythology about the 1700 subduction zone earthquake and tsunami, this book profiles a wide range of notable disasters. Some are world famous, such as the 1980 eruption of Mount St. Helens and the 1940 collapse of the Tacoma Narrows Bridge, but many are long forgotten, such as the shipwreck of the *Pacific* near Cape Flattery on the northwest coast in 1875, which killed nearly 300 people.

The state also has been plagued by many of the same kinds of disasters that hit other parts of the country—fires, floods, windstorms, and earthquakes. In many of these incidents, the number of people injured or killed was amazingly low. For instance, no one is known to have died in the Great Seattle Fire

*Ellensburg, one of three Washington cities that burned
during the summer of 1889.*
YAKIMA VALLEY MUSEUM

of 1889, even though many narrowly escaped and lost all of their possessions, as the inferno raged through the rugged business district in what was then the second-largest town in Washington Territory.

In many cases the loss of life was minimized by a stroke of luck and good timing. Fifty-seven people died on a Sunday morning in 1980 under the onslaught of the eruption of Mount St. Helens, but the loss of life would have been much greater had the mountain erupted on a Monday, when more than a thousand loggers and foresters would have been in the area that was devastated by the eruption's lateral blast. And if the eruption had hit one day earlier, hundreds of homeowners, allowed to return to their properties

Rescue and recovery efforts after the 1910 avalanche near Stevens Pass.
COURTESY UNIVERSITY OF WASHINGTON LIBRARIES. SPECIAL COLLECTIONS DIVISION, A. CURTIS 17465

close to the volcano to retrieve belongings, would have been in harm's way.

But there were disasters where timing and bad luck led to even greater loss of life. On a Fourth of July morning in 1900, in Tacoma an overloaded trolley car suffered a catastrophic brake failure and jumped the tracks, sending it hurtling off a trestle and into a ravine, killing forty-two. And in one of the worst rail disasters in U.S. history, ninety-six people died in the 1910 Wellington avalanche near Stevens Pass, when a train was trapped for days by heavy snow that blocked the tracks, leaving the passengers and crew unable to move from underneath the shadow of steep mountains.

When an avalanche predictably broke loose on March 1, it sent the entire train and its passengers tumbling down the mountainside. This incident caused the greatest loss of life for any natural disaster in Washington's history since settlers arrived.

As you read through this chronologically organized book, you will likely note the progression and grouping of similar disasters that track the maturity of Washington's changing society and economy, from the summer of burning cities in 1889, when Seattle, Ellensburg, and Spokane burned to the ground within a two-month period, to the era of shipwrecks, when in two notable incidents that took place between 1904 and 1906, more than ninety people died in the wrecks of the SS *Clallam* and the SS *Dix*. As the era of marine travel transitioned into the time of air travel, the disasters shifted to the skies with the navy plane collision over Seattle in 1937 and the crash of a plane loaded with forty-six marines into Mount Rainier in 1946.

A number of these disasters also serve as markers in the collective history of long-time Washingtonians. Anyone who is old enough to remember recalls the howling winds of the Columbus Day storm in 1962 because the storm affected such a wide swath of the state. And for a younger audience, many remember exactly where they were and what they were doing when they heard about or witnessed the eruption of Mount St. Helens.

Why write about disasters, especially in the wake of one of the worst disasters in American history—Hurricane Katrina and the flooding of New Orleans? Why focus on the sometimes awful, terrible events of our lives and histories? Quite simply because these events define us as a people and as individuals. It is these events that open our hearts to each other. And, sad and horrible as these events may be, they open our hearts to the hope that no matter what happens, we can and *do* lift ourselves up with the help of our neighbors and loved ones. In the midst of anguish, we become either our worst or best selves.

WHEN THUNDERBIRD BATTLED WHALE

The Great Cascadia Subduction Zone Earthquake

1700

It took nearly 300 years to unravel the mystery of one of Washington's earliest disasters. Native-American legends tell the story. "There was a shaking, jumping up and trembling of the earth beneath, and a rolling up of the great waters," notes a 2001 *Seattle Post-Intelligencer* account of the stories told by the Hoh and Quileute Indians along Washington's North Coast.

On January 26, 1700, between 9 and 10 P.M., the world turned upside down for tribal villagers from the Makah tribe in the north to the Chinook tribe in the south. Entire forests died in an instant, the ground dropped more than 4 feet in a moment, and giant waves lashed the coast following an earthquake with a Richter magnitude of 9.0 or larger. Imagine the residents of the coastal villages, settling into sleep in their cedar long houses, when, suddenly, violent shaking startles them out of rest. The shaking brought the collapse of long houses and huts. Within minutes after the shaking stopped, a tsunami—much like the 2004 disaster that struck along the shores of the Indian Ocean, near Indonesia, killing more than 200,000 people—would have swept inland with waves between 20 and 90 feet high. Anyone unable to reach high ground before the waves struck would have been battered by the rushing water; many villagers would have been carried out to sea.

As they did with most remarkable and inexplicable events, tribal villagers retold the story of that January night until it became part of their ancestral myths and legends, like those tales of a northern California tribe that tell of elders who sent youngsters from their village into the hills following the quake. When these youngsters returned to the village, they found that everything had been destroyed and washed away by the tsunami.

On the other side of the Pacific Ocean, Japanese villagers, who for centuries had been keeping written records of tsunami and the earthquakes that caused them, documented a 10-foot-high tsunami that struck the islands and killed villagers along the coast while sweeping the villages into the ocean. The Japanese long noted the unusual circumstances of this particular tsunami—it was the wave without an earthquake, and it damaged much of the island nation's east coast. Back on the Washington coast, the battle between shifting earth and pounding waves likely played out over days and months after the initial shock. Such a large earthquake would cause violent shaking lasting for minutes. Geologists suspect that is exactly what happened during this quake, which dropped portions of the ground along the shores of Grays Harbor as much as 4 feet.

It wasn't until the 1980s that Native-American myths, historic Japanese documents, and science came together to assemble the pieces of this remarkable puzzle. It was then that scientists in Washington began to look for the reason that thousands of western red cedar trees along the coast from Copalis in the north to the Columbia River in the south died at the same time, as determined by carbon-dating techniques. Tying that information with geological evidence, scientists came up with the theory that a major earthquake caused the trees to perish. The final piece of evidence—nailing down the year, day, and even the hour of the earthquake—was the writings from Japan about the phantom tsunami.

Geologist Brian Atwater and his colleagues continued to research Washington's coastal lowlands through soil studies, and, along with evidence of the 1700 quake, they have found evidence of at least six other subduction zone quakes—occurring when the Juan de Fuca plate breaks loose and slides under the North American plate with tremendous force—that shook the Washington coast over the past 3,500 years. Each of these quakes appears to occur over 300- to 600-year intervals, which can be traced from *subsidence*—instances where the soil levels along the coast suddenly drop below the water level, killing trees in the area. Scientists have also found thin layers of sand deposited from tsunamis buried between layers of muddy deposits that settled in the periods between earthquakes.

These subduction zone earthquakes occur in an area off the Washington shore on a line that stretches from Vancouver Island in the north to northern California in the south. The line denotes where the Juan de Fuca plate pushes underneath the North America plate. Huge earthquakes like the Cascadia Subduction Zone quake of 1700 jolt the earth when the two

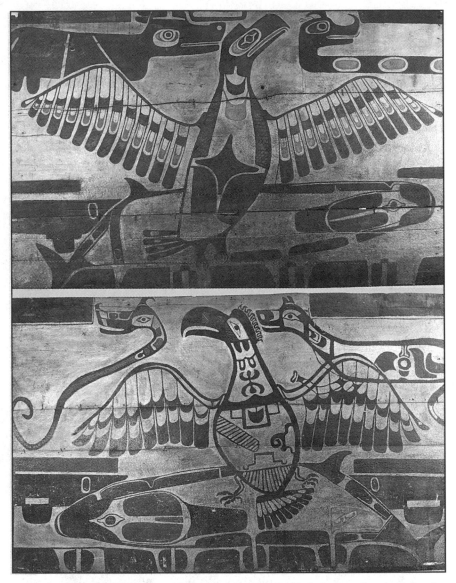

Many Pacific Northwest tribes depict an epic battle between a thunderbird and a whale that scientists believe describes a massive earthquake and tsunami. A Quileute drawing includes a waxing moon in the center, which would coincide with the lunar phase on the night of the Cascadia quake of January 26, 1700.

plates lock together and pressure builds up and then suddenly breaks loose, buckling the earth and sending ground waves out from the epicenter. Some of the largest recorded earth-quakes—such as the 2004 quake near Indonesia—occur in subduction zones.

The cyclic nature of the subduction zone earthquakes may explain the prevalence of Native-American legends about the fierce battles between Thunderbird and Whale. We retell the tale for you here (based on several tales we have been told or read):

> Whale roamed the ocean eating all the food. Whale was greedy, and the people were starving because he ate all the food. But Thunderbird looked down from her great aerie and saw that Whale was not sharing. Thunderbird flew down to the ocean and dove after Whale. Whale and Thunderbird fought in the waters and caused great splash-ing. The waters left the ocean and leapt onto the land and swallowed many people and their canoes. Finally, Thunder-bird pulled Whale from the water and flew back to her nest. Whale was heavy and thrashed in the air, making Thunderbird drop him, and the earth shook. They fought again on the ground, and the earth shook more. Thunder-bird took Whale to her nest and the earth stopped shaking, and the waters were calm, and the people once again fished in the ocean and were no longer hungry.

Some tribal stories talk of the ground or sand shifting and failing underfoot; other tales of tell of many deaths and canoes strewn in the trees following great floods. Yet others talk of creatures stomping on the earth or throwing down boulders to cause the earth to shake. Ethnologists believe that many of these stories can be linked to other earthquakes—just as the story of the maiden Loowit and her suitors Wy'east and Pahto record the geological rumblings and fireworks of Mount St. Helens, Mount Hood, and Mount Adams. Even today, we create our own myths about earthquakes, tsunami, and volcanoes. Ask anyone who lived through an earthquake and stories will come.

Geologists warn that another quake of an equal or greater magnitude than the 1700 earthquake could hit the Washington coast at any time. Only time will tell when Thunderbird and Whale will battle once more.

GRAVEYARD OF THE PACIFIC

The Columbia River Bar
1841–1936

Few river entrances in the world carry the same mystique and command as much respect for the forces of nature as does the entrance to the Columbia River. The combination of swirling currents, winds, and sandbars at the entrance to the West Coast's largest river have caused more than 2,000 shipwrecks and claimed more than 700 lives since the days of the Lewis and Clark Expedition. Due to these statistics, the Columbia River bar ranks as one of the most dangerous river entrances in the world.

It's useful to keep a few facts in mind when considering how the bar can be such a treacherous place. First, as one of the largest rivers in the United States, the Columbia River carries a tremendous current—between 90,000 and 1 million cubic feet per second—into the Pacific Ocean. Even today, with the river slowed by one of the largest networks of dams in the world, the current at the mouth of the Columbia is exceedingly strong. Over the centuries this current has carried rocks and sand downstream from the source of the river in Canada all the way to the ocean, and these deposits are the major contributors to the sandbars at the mouth of the river, as well as the major spits that jut into the ocean on each side of the river mouth— Clatsop Spit on the Oregon side to the south and Peacock Spit on the Washington side to the north. When these sands are deposited at the mouth of the river, wave action from the Pacific Ocean meets with the river's current to cause the shifting deposits to pile up into sandbars, restricting the deep channels that are needed for ships entering the river.

Against this shifting backdrop, the opposing forces of the Columbia River's current mingling with the force of storm-driven waves from the Pacific Ocean regularly cause rough seas along the bar, with waves that frequently build to more than 30 or 40 feet, and even higher seas in extreme storms.

A 411-foot steamer named the SS *Iowa* ventured into these turbulent conditions with thirty-four crew members aboard on a stormy night on January 11, 1936. According to an account of the shipwreck in David H. Grover's book *The Unforgiving Coast: Maritime Disasters of the Pacific Northwest,* the *Iowa* had just finished taking on a load of lumber at a Weyerhaeuser dock in Longview, when it steamed toward the Pacific Ocean carrying more than 6,900 long tons of cargo, including nearly 2.5 million board feet of lumber. No sooner had the ship crossed the Columbia River bar around midnight than a gale estimated at 75 miles per hour hit the region and buffeted the ship as its captain tried to battle the opposing forces of current, waves, and wind. Capt. Edgar Yates had crossed the river bar more than 200 times, and he opted not to use a bar pilot on this crossing. But this time as the ship crossed the bar, it turned broadside to the incoming seas and heavy winds. A Coast Guard observer at the Cape Disappointment Lighthouse watched the *Iowa* as it cleared a navigational buoy and started to turn south near the end of the South Jetty, but he recalled after the wreck that the ship inexplicably turned to the north toward Peacock Spit around 2 A.M. As the observer watched through increasingly stormy conditions, the *Iowa* appeared oblivious to the danger as it approached the spit, where water depths were around 20 feet—the ship needed an average water depth of 22 feet to clear the spit. At around 4:30 A.M. a Coast Guard station in Astoria reported hearing an SOS call from the *Iowa*—the ship had run aground.

The situation onboard the *Iowa* must have turned desperate as soon as it ran aground. The radio transmissions stopped as soon as the ship lodged on the spit. Observers at the Cape Disappointment Lighthouse tried to contact the ship using light signals, and they did see a brief signal in response, but they were unable to decipher the message. As the Coast Guard cutter *Onondaga* tried to rush through rough seas to the scene of the wreck, the observers at Cape Disappointment tried hoisting flags to communicate with the crippled ship. Onboard the *Iowa* a few flags were raised in response, but once again the conditions were too poor to decipher the meaning of the flags. There was no way to reach the ship and try to save the vessel or its crew. As observers watched through telescopes, they saw a crew member trying to make his way toward the foremast when a huge wave broke over the deck and washed him overboard. Moments later, another wave wiped the pilothouse from the ship.

When the *Onondaga* arrived on the scene two hours later, there weren't any signs of life, and only the masts protruded above the waves. All thirty-four crew members were gone, and only six bodies were recovered in the following days.

The wreck of the *Iowa* was much like other ships that fell victim to Peacock Spit. The sandbar earned its name on July 18, 1841, when the U.S. Navy sloop the USS *Peacock* ran aground on the spit while attempting to report for duty as part of the Wilkes Expedition to explore the Pacific Northwest coast. The 118-foot, three-masted ship under the command of U.S. Navy lieutenant William Hudson tried to enter the Columbia River using sailing directions that were given to him by the captain of a merchant ship encountered earlier in the year in Hawaii, but by the time the *Peacock* attempted crossing, the sand spit at the river's mouth had moved.

Once the ship was aground, the *Peacock*'s crew tried to regain control of the situation and get the eighteen-gun vessel off the sand spit, but waves repeatedly picked up the ship and slammed it back down onto the sand, accompanied by the sounds of cracking timbers. After fighting to free the ship for hours, Hudson ordered crew members to fire flares and try to attract the attention of nearby boats. Eventually, boats came to the aid of, and evacuated, the entire crew. No one died in the incident, and the Wilkes Expedition continued its work, which included navigating the Columbia River as far inland as the Cascade Mountains. But the *Peacock* was done. The spit on which it wrecked and broke apart has been known as Peacock Spit ever since.

Following decades of treacherous shipwrecks along the Columbia River bar, beginning in 1884 the United States Corps of Engineers undertook the mammoth task of building a jetty on the south side of the river mouth, to help flush sand out into the ocean and keep a navigable channel open for shipping interests. A north jetty was started in 1914, and together the jetties helped make the Columbia River bar a little more

*Peacock Spit was named for an eighteen-gun vessel that
wrecked there in heavy surf in 1841, as depicted in this engraving
of the abandonment of the* Peacock.
DEPARTMENT OF THE NAVY—NAVAL HISTORICAL CENTER, ALFRED AGATE COLLECTION

manageable. Advances in ship propulsion also made a difference, as ships transitioned from wind power to steam driven
stern-wheelers and side-wheelers and then to vessels powered
by combustion engines. Other technological improvements,
like radio communications and modern navigation equipment, also reduced the chance of a shipwreck.

Despite these efforts, the Columbia River bar continues to
demand respect. It is the only river bar in the United States
that requires a bar pilot to guide ships through the shallow,
churning waters. Even today with depth finders and global
positioning systems, shoals can appear abruptly.

The shipwreck of the tanker *Rosencrans* on January 7, 1913, further illustrates why there is no room for error when entering

the mouth of the Columbia River. According to the account described in *Pacific Graveyard* by James A. Gibbs Jr., it was dark on the morning of January 7, when the captain of the ill-fated *Rosencrans* started toward the bar en route to Portland with 20,000 barrels of crude oil. According to the three members of the thirty-three member crew who survived the morning, the ship's captain, L. F. Johnson, mistook the North Head Lighthouse signal for the signal of the lightship—a stationary ship anchored and manned as a navigation point—near Clatsop Spit. By the time he realized the mistake, the *Rosencrans* slammed into the tip of Peacock Spit in 60-mile-per-hour winds. A radioman on the stranded ship called for help at 5:15 A.M., but by the time anyone could respond, the huge ship had split in two.

Members of the crew who survived the first part of the wreck and the splitting apart of the ship were forced to scramble into the rigging to escape the raging sea, as the rest of the ship sank into a frothy mix of oil and saltwater. More than 18,000 barrels of oil burst from the *Rosencrans*'s hold and coated the wave tops before soiling beaches from Cape Disappointment to North Head. By the time a surf boat approached the wreck, just three crew members were riding the rigging. One of those three crew members fell from the mast and drowned before he could be pulled from the water, but ship carpenter Erick Lindmark and quartermaster Joseph Stenning were plucked from the wreckage. A third crew member, Fred Peters, survived by riding a plank from the wreck through the breakers and onto the shore near Tioga on the North Beach peninsula—nearly 17 miles from the wreck of the *Rosencrans*. "The plank wasn't very big, only about 4 feet long, a foot wide and 2 inches thick, but, let me tell you, it did me a lot of good," Peters said in an article in the *Oregonian*. Peters described being washed overboard by a wave as the *Rosencrans* was breaking up, and that he somehow propelled himself toward the shore.

Peters was one of the lucky few among those washed overboard on the Columbia River bar. Although epic shipwrecks are no longer common at the river's entrance, mariners continue to respect the power and unpredictability of the Columbia River bar.

CHAPTER 3

FRESH PAINT HIDES A ROTTEN HULL

The Wreck of the *Pacific*
1875

With fondly ling'ring thoughts the maiden waves
Her Kerchief flag of tender, mute farewell.
While on the chilly breeze floats soft and low
Her parting strain—"Good bye, sweetheart, good bye!"
—From "Ode on the Loss of the Steamship *Pacific*"
by George Mason

On November 4, 1875—fourteen years before Washington became a state—the recently refurbished side-wheeler *Pacific* steamed to Victoria under the command of a young, promising captain, J. D. Howell. Howell, who was only thirty-four years old, was a former Confederate sailor who had commanded the *Pacific* for less than three months. He had grounded his last charge on Tillamook Head, but his heroic leadership ensured no lives were lost. The *Pacific* started its voyage in Tacoma and stopped at other Puget Sound ports, picking up passengers and cargo. At Victoria passengers streamed onto Howell's ship, and the crew loaded its cargo.

The passenger manifest listed tourists, businessmen, and miners who were returning home from the Cassiar gold fields. In fact Richard Lyons and Dennis Cain struck it rich looking for gold and were returning to San Francisco in a first-class cabin. J. H. Sullivan, the gold commissioner from the Cassiar fields, was also journeying south. Perhaps Mason wrote the lines that open this story about Fannie Palmer, a popular young woman from Victoria who may have had more than one beau waving to her from the wharf as she left to visit her sister in California. The ship was overloaded with freight and passengers, including some passengers who leaped aboard as castaways when the ship began to pull away from the wharf. The *Pacific* held berths for 200 passengers, but far more tickets had been sold. Considerably more than 250 people were onboard, including walk-on passengers who were not on the passenger list, crew members, and as many as forty-one unlisted Chinese laborers. Some accounts claim that as many as 300 people were onboard the *Pacific* on its final, fatal voyage.

The ship hobbled out of port with a starboard list at 9:30 A.M. But the passengers and onlookers weren't worried. They were impressed by the sharp-looking steamer. The *Pacific* looked brand new. The owners, Goodall, Nelson & Perkins Steamship Company, said that they had spent more than $40,000 refurbishing it. But the beauty was only skin deep, as events that were soon to unfold proved.

Soon after the wooden, three-masted, steam-powered sidewheeler was built in New York in 1850, it broke a speed record on its first voyage to New Orleans. However, although it was fast, the ship had a narrow 30-foot beam for its 225-foot length and a capacity of only 876 tons. The ship changed hands several times and ended up on the West Coast in 1851, making the San Francisco-Panama and then the San Francisco-Columbia River run. In July 1861, when the steamer was on its way from Portland to Astoria, Oregon, it hit Coffin Rock (a former Native-American burial ground that was later destroyed and used to pave the streets of Portland and build the jetty at the mouth of the Columbia River) near modern-day Longview, Washington, where it sank. After the ship spent a few days at the bottom of the river, it was raised, and a fire engine was shipped from Portland to pump the water out of the hold before the ship was repaired and put back into service.

The ship was retired and stored on the mudflats around San Francisco with other decrepit steamers in 1872, the same year that gold was found in the Cassiar gold district. By 1874 miners were striking it rich—or not—and were returning to their homes in California and across the nation. And they needed transportation. As a result greedy steamship operators snatched up anything that floated, or almost floated; made a few cosmetic repairs; and again pressed them into service running freight and people between San Francisco and Victoria, British Columbia, as well as other stops along the Strait of Juan de Fuca and Puget Sound. The *Pacific* received a gloss of new paint and shiny brass fixtures, but the wood beneath the paint was rotten and brittle. Shipbuilders who worked on the ship in San Francisco claimed that they could easily push tools through the spongy wood.

Although no clear explanation has been offered for the starboard list as the ship left Victoria Harbor, most people assume that improperly loaded cargo was to blame, and the ship did carry a lot of it, including 2,000 sacks of oats, 280 tons of coal, and 28 tons of merchandise and sundries. It also carried two cases of opium, two buggies, and thirty-one barrels of cranberries—the last most likely to be eaten within the next few weeks at Thanksgiving feasts. By the time the crew loaded the last of the freight, the lower holds were full, and the crew lashed some of the cargo to the top deck. The ship also carried $80,000 worth of gold for Wells Fargo and six show horses and two dogs that were part of the Rockwell & Hurlbert Equestrian Troupe, which just finished its West Coast tour— the six human members of the troupe were also onboard. The crew scrambled to adjust and balance the load, but their efforts proved inadequate. At one point they asked the passengers to move to one side of the boat in order to counter the list. Eventually, some lifeboats were partially filled with water to bring the ship into even keel. It took the *Pacific* more than six and a half hours before it finally made it out of the Strait of Juan de Fuca to Cape Flattery, where the ship was greeted by a rising gale.

> *The rush, the panic—accents of despair,—*
> *The infant's wail,—the Mother's piercing cry—*
> *The brave man's fight with death, and chivalry*
> *Unselfish even to his latest gasp.*

At 8 P.M. twenty-one-year-old quartermaster Neil Henley, who had only been in the United States since August, transferred the helm to the night watch and headed down to his bunk in the forecastle for the night. Two hours later, he woke to a loud sound. He rose quickly and was surprised to find water pouring through a large hole in the hull. By the time he reached the deck, passengers were crowding so near the lifeboats that crew members were having problems maneuvering them.

While Henley slept, the *Pacific* had continued its voyage south while the square-rigger *Orpheus,* carrying only ballast, headed north toward Nanaimo, British Columbia, to pick up a load of coal to take back to San Francisco. Capt. Charles A. Sawyer had just left the *Orpheus* in the hands of the second mate, while he went to his cabin to study his charts. He was trying to determine how close the entrance to the strait was. He told the second mate that if he saw anything he should pull to starboard. Almost as soon as Sawyer sat down, the ship shifted course. Sawyer went back to the deck where the mate told him he had seen the Flattery light off of port, his sea side. Sawyer knew that there was no way that the lighthouse would be on that side of his ship, and when Sawyer looked, he saw the light now off to starboard and brought his ship to a near standstill. He thought the approaching ship would surely see him and change course, but the *Pacific* did not see the *Orpheus* in time to avert disaster. Just before the ships glanced off each other, the *Pacific* blew its whistle once in warning.

The collision was not direct; it was more like two cars in a narrow alley scraping sides. Nevertheless, it ripped much of the starboard rigging off of the *Orpheus,* enough so that Sawyer was concerned for a short time for the safety of his ship and crew. Sawyer did call to the *Pacific* because he needed assistance for his injured boat, but no reply was forthcoming. Sawyer's wife, who had joined him on deck, was about to jump onto the *Pacific,* but Sawyer grabbed her in time and, unknown to him at the time, saved her from what would have been certain death. Assuming that the light blow had not damaged the other ship, he turned his attention to his own ship and sailed

*Top: The lighthouse at Tatoosh Island with Cape Flattery and the
entrance to the Straits of Juan de Fuca seen in the center right.
Bottom: Flattery Rocks, approximately 12 nautical miles south of Cape Flattery.*
FROM *PACIFIC COAST: COAST PILOT OF CALIFORNIA, OREGON, AND WASHINGTON TERRITORY,*
BY GEORGE DAVIDSON, 1869. ARCHIVAL PHOTOGRAPHY BY STEVE NICKLAS, NOAA CENTRAL LIBRARY

on. It only took about fifteen minutes for Sawyer to realize his
ship was in no real danger and to look back for the *Pacific.*
When he saw no lights behind him, he again assumed the ship
was safe and continued on his way.

Onboard the *Pacific,* Jennie Parsons was sobbing with grief
as she stepped into the lifeboat. She was sailing to San
Francisco along with her eighteen-month-old baby; her husband, Capt. Otis Parsons; and her sister, brother, and sister-in-
law. Just before she made it to the lifeboat, her baby was
crushed to death in the press of the crowd. The crew eventually

succeeded in launching the lifeboat loaded with women, children, and a handful of men, including Neil Henley and passenger Henry Jelly. But the lifeboat had been used to balance the ship and was filled with water. It capsized immediately. None of the Parsons family was ever seen alive again. However, Jelly struggled back to the surface and climbed on top of the lifeboat along with three other men, and Henley grabbed onto a skylight that floated near him and used it to keep himself afloat.

Within minutes they heard the timbers of the *Pacific* cracking as the ship broke apart before quickly sinking from sight, taking most of the passengers with it. Henley and Jelly heard the moans and death cries of passengers for a short time, before the cold and water silenced them. The winter water temperatures around Cape Flattery hover around forty-five degrees and are known to dip into the thirties. At those temperatures hypothermia sets in quickly, hands grow numb and are unable to grasp flotation devices: Drowning is unavoidable unless a person is wearing a life jacket, and most of the people on the *Pacific* did not have time to don them. Somehow Jelly was able to make it from the boat to a section of the pilothouse along with another survivor. Henley eventually found part of the hurricane deck and climbed on. Captain Howell, the cook, the second mate, four male passengers, and one female passenger were already on the makeshift raft.

By first light the captain, second mate, woman, and one male passenger had been washed away from the hurricane deck. Henley estimated that it was around 9 A.M. when the cook died and rolled off. Meanwhile Jelly snagged some passing life jackets, cut the ropes from them, and used those ropes to lash himself and the other gentlemen to the pilothouse. At some point that day, the people on the hurricane deck saw land about 15 miles away and then saw two men floating on some debris. One can only guess that it was the pilothouse with Jelly onboard. Unfortunately, the other man, whose name Jelly either never learned or was unable to recall, died that afternoon. Jelly cut him loose and pushed him off into the sea.

By 5 P.M. Henley and a passenger were the only survivors on the hurricane deck. Both men survived the night, barely clinging to the deck. The passenger died early the next morning, which left Henley alone. At about 8 A.M., the passing bark *Messenger* found Jelly, and by that afternoon, Jelly was safe in Port Townsend, where the rest of the world began to learn of the disaster. Meanwhile, Henley found a box, pulled it onto the deck, and used it to block the wind while he slept. Henley spent the day and the next night watching the sea pass by and occasionally sleeping while the waves and wind battered the hurricane deck. Finally, on the morning of November 8, more than eighty hours after the collision, the U.S. revenue cutter *Oliver Wolcott* plucked Henley, near death, from the deck. On its way back to sea, the *Wolcott* found the *Orpheus* wrecked at Barclay Sound on the rocky west coast of Vancouver Island—luckily the crew survived the mishap.

At first people did not believe Jelly's story. It was simply too hard for them to believe that more than 250 people died in a few short moments onboard what was supposed to be a newly remodeled ship. However, when Henley repeated the same story, residents of the Pacific coast from Victoria, British Columbia, to San Francisco, California, began to realize the enormity of the disaster. So many people were crammed onboard the *Pacific* that nearly everyone in Victoria was related to or knew someone who died, and they began to turn their ire toward the master of the *Orpheus*. He, after all, had ignored the

law of the sea and had left the site of a collision before ensuring that all onboard the other ship were safe. The final insult
came to the city when the beautiful young Fannie Palmer
washed up just miles from her home—40 miles from where
the *Pacific* sank.

No one could think of a more fitting epitaph for the wreck
of the *Pacific* than that written by Sewell Moody, a wealthy
sawmill owner who took a berth on the ship en route to a busi
ness meeting in San Francisco. Sometime during the night of
November 4 he had taken a pencil out of his pocket and had
written on a scrap of the ship, "All lost. S. P. Moody." The
scrap, on display at the Vancouver Maritime Museum, is all
that is left of this worst of the Pacific coast maritime disasters.
Even the memory of that awful night has almost slipped into
oblivion, with few left to cry:

> But hush—again! the news! the dreadful news
> Has reached our shores! has paralyzed the hearts
> Of all! Oh! say; it is not true! What! lost!
> All lost! All! All! . . .

A CITY IN FLAMES

The Great Seattle Fire
1889

The nearly 25,000 residents of Seattle were enjoying another in a string of warm days on the afternoon of June 6, 1889. It was a dry spring—a pleasant break from the never-ending rain that can dominate spring weather in Seattle.

Already a bustling city with a rapidly growing number of wood buildings and boardwalks, Seattle was primed to be the center of commerce for Washington Territory when it would become a state at the end of 1889. But Seattle's history took a turn late in the afternoon of June 6.

John E. Back, a Swedish emigrant to the United States and a recent arrival in Seattle, was hard at work in the basement of the Clairmont and Company cabinet shop on Front Street and Madison Avenue that afternoon. As an assistant in Victor Clairmont's woodworking shop, it was Back's duty to prepare a batch of glue for the afternoon's cabinet making by heating it over a gasoline fire. He stepped away from the fire for a moment—and that was all it took to start the Great Seattle Fire.

Back told his story to a *Seattle Post-Intelligencer* reporter in an issue published June 21, 1889:

I cut some balls of glue and put them in the glue pot on the
stove . . . [and] went to work about twenty-five feet away, near
the front door. After a while somebody said "Look at the
glue." Another fellow, a Finlander from New York, then took
a piece of board and laid it on to smother the glue, but the
board caught fire. Then I run and took the pot of water to
smother the fire and poured it over the pot of glue, which
was blazing up high. When I throw the water on, the glue
flew all over the shop into the shavings and everything take
fire.

The mixture of burning glue, wood shavings, and turpen-
tine served as a potent accelerant as the fire spread from the
cabinet shop. The fire started shortly after 2:15 P.M. and raced
from the cabinet shop to neighboring buildings with rapid
intensity. The nearby Dietz & Mayor Liquor Store exploded in
alcohol-fueled flames that next engulfed the Crystal Palace
Saloon and the Opera House Saloon. The alcohol added to the
conflagration, and soon the entire city block from Marion to
Madison was in flames. According to a woman who witnessed
the fire:

There was a big crowd. Half the people in town were down
there. The man who started the fire was a roomer in our
house, and his name was John Back. He was the one that
started the fire. And they were going to lynch him if they
found him.

Harriet Case, whose father J. D. Gardner owned the Rice
and Gardner meat market, was at school when the fire began.
She wrote about the event in *Told by the Pioneers:*

A few minutes before school was dismissed at 3 o'clock, we heard the fire bell. I thought it was quite a fire as the fire bell kept ringing continuously. . . . I was 14 years old then, and when I heard the fire bells I ran to see what it was about.

Harriet ran to her father's shop as the fire advanced toward it. He gave her a black dispatch box filled with all of the shop's important papers and told her to take it home for safekeeping.

The fire continued to spread from the initial block, burning underneath the buildings. Wooden boardwalks served as conduits to carry the flames from one side of the road to the other and out of sight of the city's crews of volunteer firefighters as they arrived on the scene. To make matters worse, when firefighters tried to use the water supply from the Spring Hill Water Company, there was little water pressure. The wood fire hydrants on every other street burned along with the wooden water pipes as the fire advanced. Seattle mayor Robert Moran took control of the fire department from substitute fire chief James Murphy—the city's fire chief, Josiah Collins, was at a firefighting convention in San Francisco when the fire struck—and under Moran's command the firefighters worked to blow up entire city blocks in a desperate effort to create a firebreak and stop the spread of the flames. The Colman block was blown up first, but windy conditions and the endless supply of wood used in boardwalks and building materials helped the fire bridge that firebreak. Meanwhile the flames marched down to the wharves, where they destroyed anything in their path, including goods and supplies that townspeople had moved to the water's edge in hopes of loading them onto ships to float beyond the reach of the flames. "Attempts to save personal property met with only partial success," wrote James

This photo, taken in the vicinity of Pioneer Square,
shows a city destroyed by fire.
UNIVERSITY OF WASHINGTON LIBRARIES, SPECIAL COLLECTIONS, UW 6991

Warren in the book, *King County and Its Emerald City: Seattle.*
"If piled in the streets, it was usually consumed by the flames.
Goods transported to the wharves were also burned except for
what little was loaded on two steamships and moved out into
Elliott Bay."

Seattleites could sense that the downtown business core of
the city was doomed within ninety minutes of the fire's start.
They hustled to clear goods from stores and offices in advance
of the flames, saving what they could as they went. Writing in
the June 10, 1889, edition of the *Seattle Times,* newspapermen
described how their offices had been consumed and offered
hopeful notes for the future. "The *Times* office went up in the
flames, nothing being saved but the reporters, the files and a

The ravaged buildings shown are the Post, Yesler-Leary,
and Occidental on the left and the Colman on the right.
PHOTO BY JOHN P. SOULE, UNIVERSITY OF WASHINGTON LIBRARIES, SPECIAL COLLECTIONS, UW 2300

few other minor implements of the trade," said a first-page
article published following the fire, under the header: "Slightly
disfigured, but still in the ring! This is the song Seattle will
sing. New buildings, new hopes, new streets, new town!
There's nothing that Seattle can throw down. She goes through
adversity, fire and flame: But the Queen City gets there just the
same."

Louis S. Rice was the co-owner of the Rice and Gardner
meat market. Mr. Rice was in eastern Washington buying cattle when the fire began, but Melissa Rice, his wife, went to the
shop and, along with Mr. Gardner and the other workers, took
the meat to the family home, located at Fifth and Madison.
There they dumped the meat, along with the furniture from

the Gardners' home at Third and Yesler, in the yard. Rice recalled the day in an essay he wrote for *Told by the Pioneers:* "The two women cooked meat all day long for the fire fighters and the people who had lost everything in the disaster. All of the butchers and meat cutters came there to eat."

As the fire rushed up the hill to consume Second Avenue and then raced toward Third Avenue, firefighters hosed down the three-story courthouse building with what meager water pressure they had left. The building appeared to be doomed, since the water could only reach the first floor, but in a brilliant move, a man named Lawrence Booth organized a bucket brigade to take buckets of water to the roof of the courthouse and douse the sides of the building from there. His quick thinking and improvisation saved the building from the flames and inspired others in neighboring blocks to try the same trick, which helped save the Boston block and Jacob Levy's house. In another variation someone covered the outside of Henry Yesler's house with wet blankets and saved it from the greedy flames as well.

With this handful of exceptions, the fire marched through Seattle's downtown unabated. Firefighters tried blowing up another block to create a firebreak, but once again the fire marched on and burned through the tinder-dry wood along Skid Road. The fire bells continued to ring through the long day. As Harriet Case recalled, "The bells of the Episcopal and Catholic church were tolling along with the fire bell, sounding as though everybody was dying." Nearly six hours after the fire started, Mayor Moran declared an 8 P.M. curfew to keep looters off the streets and ordered all saloons closed until further notice.

The magnitude of the destruction made it more feasible to rebuild the city just about from scratch. This image shows First Avenue from Columbia Street, looking southwest.

PHOTO BY JOHN P. SOULE, UNIVERSITY OF WASHINGTON LIBRARIES, SPECIAL COLLECTIONS, UW 5947

The fire continued to burn until 3 A.M., leaving a path of destruction that included 25 city blocks and more than one hundred acres. The financial loss was estimated at roughly $8 million, but there was no record after the fire of anyone dying in the flames. The city's business core was destroyed, and along with it an estimated one million rats were thought to have died in the fire!

Seattle started picking up the pieces on June 7, 1889. Mayor Moran held a meeting with members of the business community and discussed options for reconstruction. The majority of businesses planned to rebuild, but it was agreed that no wooden buildings would be built in the fire's footprints. It was also agreed that Seattle needed a full-time fire-fighting force to replace the volunteer firefighters who tried and failed to stop the raging inferno a day earlier.

James Warren's book on Seattle includes this quote from the June 7 meeting: "Jacob Furth spoke for those present when he said: 'The time is not far distant when we shall look upon the fire as an actual benefit. I say we shall have a finer city than before, not within five years, but in eighteen months.'" Furth's prediction was fairly accurate. At the time of the fire, Seattle was actually a smaller city than Tacoma, located to the south, but within a year of the fire Seattle became the biggest city in Washington with a population that expanded from 25,000 residents before the fire to 40,000 residents after it. The city's business core was rebuilt using brick rather than wood, in an effort to ensure that a repeat fire would be less likely. Designers also created the Seattle underground in the rebuilding effort by building the streets and entrances to buildings one to two stories higher than the ground level.

While Seattle's fate took a turn for the better following the dramatic fire, one Seattle resident had his life turned upside down. In initial reports following the fire, the *Seattle Post-Intelligencer* mistakenly pinned the blame for the fire on one James McGough, and although the *P-I* issued a correction in the June 21, 1889, edition, the mistake echoed through historical accounts over the years. As the years ticked by, McGough made an annual appeal to remind people that the fire did not start in his paint shop, but the story continues to show up in articles about the great fire. McGough's personal part in the Great Seattle Fire ended on the streets of Seattle on January 20, 1910, when the painting contractor was run down and killed by a speeding streetcar.

CHAPTER 5

A PHOENIX FROM THE ASHES

The Great Spokane Falls Fire
1889

What appeared to be tragedy on August 4, 1889, turned out to be a tale of the Phoenix rising from the ashes of the Great Spokane Falls Fire. On a hot summer Sunday evening, over the course of four hours, 32 city blocks and the core of the city of Spokane Falls burned to the ground, but the fire proved to be the catapult that was needed to launch Spokane toward becoming Washington's second-largest city.

That future was not on anyone's mind on the evening of August 4, 1889, when the fire started around 6 P.M. The origin of the blaze is still open for debate. One popular theory says that lunchroom owner Bill Wolfe triggered the blaze when pork chops he was cooking on a stovetop sparked a small kitchen fire that spread to a greasy towel and then engulfed the entire room. Another story attributes the fire to saloon girl "Irish Kate." As the story goes, Kate was working when a drunken man came in and started an argument with her. When the fight concluded, Kate went upstairs over the saloon and decided to fix her hair. She put her curling iron into a kerosene lamp to warm. The man reappeared and the argument started all over again. During the tussle that followed, Kate fell onto the table where her iron was warming and knocked the kerosene lamp to the floor, starting the blaze.

Others believe the fire started from a spark that was thrown from a passing train, but regardless of which story you choose to believe, once the fire was started it was a force to be reckoned with, and one that would forever change the city.

Passing police officers were the first to join the patrons of the lunchroom in trying to douse the flames with buckets of water, but they couldn't bring the blaze under control. In moments the fire raced up a stairway and engulfed the entire building as people inside scrambled for their lives.

The flames quickly jumped from Bill Wolfe's lunchroom on Railroad Avenue to adjacent buildings and a call went out to Spokane Falls's volunteer firefighters to battle the blaze. Firefighters arrived quickly on the scene with their horse-drawn wagons, but as had happened earlier in the year in Seattle, when they hooked up their hoses to the city's water-works, there was no water pressure from the new hydrants. This spelled trouble for the small firefighting crew.

In the three years between 1886 and 1889, Spokane grew rapidly. Boarding houses and hotels popped up on nearly every scrap of vacant land, and open spaces between buildings were filled with buildings that crowded together in the city core. Jay J. Kalez described the changes in his book, *This Town of Ours . . . Spokane:* "In 1889 Spokane Falls had six banks, twelve black-smiths, fifteen barbers, four cigar factories, thirty groceries, ten lunch counters, sixteen restaurants, and three theaters."

Much of this new development was built quickly of tinder-dry wood, and the flames that erupted on August 4 were hungry to make quick work of burning down what had been built over the previous three years. Even if the fire hydrant system had worked as it was designed to, many historians doubt that the firefighters would have been able to stop the blaze before it had torched most of the downtown core.

As with the origin of the fire, there is some debate about why the fire hoses didn't work on that Sunday night. The most popular explanation is that Rolla A. Jones, who was in charge of the city's water system, was out of town on a fishing trip when the fire started, and no one else knew how to turn on the pumps to get water to the fire. Jones handed the keys for the water system to an assistant, but the assistant didn't know how to operate the machinery that started the pumps. As a result, firefighters scrambled in vain to find hydrants that worked. The less-popular explanation for the lack of water pressure is that workmen were working on a water main on Post Street and that they had shut off the valve at that point in the water system, stopping water from making its way to the site of the blaze on Railroad Avenue.

As the situation grew more desperate and it was clear that there was no way to get water to the fire, Spokane Falls's mayor, Fred Furth, decided that the only way to slow the fire from consuming the entire city was to blow up buildings ahead of the flames, creating a firebreak. This same tactic had been used during the Seattle fire earlier in the year. The explosions leveled the buildings on entire city blocks, but the blasts created piles of wood and rubble that burned along with the still-standing buildings. Making matters worse, winds whipped up and pushed the fire all the way to the shores of the Spokane River, where firefighters scrambled to keep the blaze from reaching two lumber mills. Firefighters had their first lucky break of the night once the fire reached the river; the winds died down and allowed them to keep the flames from licking the lumber mills.

The scene on the streets of Spokane Falls was chaotic, as people rushed to save what they could of their lives from the growing inferno. Many residents and shop owners tried to save their belongings by rushing them out into the streets, only to see the flames consume them anyway. People were paying nearly any asking price for a vehicle that could be used to try to save the most valuable items.

Real estate business owner G. W. Roche recalled the scene in an article in Ralph W. Andrews's book, *Historic Fires of the West:*

> The hoarse shouts of the men running in all directions, the shrieks of women and children, the rattle of the wagons, the tolling of church bells, the shrill whistles of locomotives as they hurried to and fro trying to save the cars lined on the N. P. tracks, the angry roar of the flames, the embers and shingles flying through the air, the explosion of giant powder [used in blowing up corner buildings in an effort to check the flames], all combined to make the night hideous in the extreme.

Washington National Guard Brig. Gen. R. G. O'Brien offered his description of the scene in a letter to the general headquarters in Olympia:

When the order was received the beautiful city of Spokane Falls was in flames. Her noble business blocks, the pride of her citizens, were crumbling to atoms before the intense heat. The wildest confusion and disorder prevailed. The lawless element, which unfortunately forms a part of the population of every prosperous city in the Northwest, in the excitement of this great calamity were unrestrained by fear of the law. The police force of the municipal Government, although as efficient as of any city in Washington, was by its limited numbers, entirely inadequate to perform the multiplicity of duties which were imposed upon it. Valuable property was abandoned with reckless indifference in order to save life.

When the fire died down and the smoke cleared, most of Spokane Falls had been converted to a charred mess. The only areas left untouched were the Crescent block and the American Theater. Two people who were unable to outrun the fire died in the conflagration. Estimates of the financial damages from the fire ranged widely between $6 million and $12 million—the latter estimate being about $4 million more than the damages caused by the Great Seattle Fire in June.

Falling on the heels of the Great Seattle Fire and the Fourth of July fire in Ellensburg just a month after that, some people looked back on the curious summer of city fires as a little too coincidental. More than one writer floated the idea of a serial arsonist who may have toured the state, starting fires as he went along. But there is little evidence to support the theory.

Tacoma Ledger writer R. F. Radebaugh explained the theory in an article called "Northwest Fire Losses Were Big":

Onlookers survey the ashes of the Ellensburg fire in July 1889.
COURTESY YAKIMA VALLEY MUSEUM (2002-802-274)

The period of preparing for the constitutional convention and admission of Washington as a state—from the spring of 1888 to the summer of 1889—was marked by such a number of large and very destructive fires in cities and towns of our territory as to arouse suspicion that they resulted from a deliberately organized plan and purpose of destruction.

This never advanced beyond being a theory. No one could connect the incidents to prove that the fires were intentionally set. And, when the scope of all the fires is considered, the theory seems even more implausible.

Spokane Falls went through major change following the fire. Shortly after the blaze, the city dropped "Falls" from its name and became Spokane. In response to the fire, Spokane went on to create its first professional firefighting force on December 18, 1889. The city established a twenty-five-member fire department with an annual budget of $33,000—a bargain compared with the cost of the blaze earlier in the year. Meanwhile, buildings made of brick and mortar took the place of the ramshackle wooden buildings that had burned so quickly in the fire.

Spokane had learned its lesson, the same lesson learned by Seattle and Ellensburg.

CHAPTER 6

A WASHINGTON WASHOUT

The Conconully Flood
1894

Today, visitors to Conconully will find a small, dusty but picturesque burg of 200 people that is best known for cattle drives,
summer fishing, hunting, and winter recreation. But in May
1894 Conconully, home to Washington's first Episcopal
church, and then-county seat for Okanogan County, was still
rebuilding itself from a series of disasters that had recently
challenged the mining town. Twenty-two months earlier, in the
early morning of August 30, 1892, fire swept through the town
when strong winds pushed flames from a new store that was
under construction to engulf buildings on both sides of the
main street. Thirty-four buildings burned, and the townspeople rebuilt. Then in 1893 a recession and drastic drop in the
price of silver forced most of the mines that had fueled
Conconully's growth to close. Many of the city's residents stuck
around in hopes that better days would return. And then came
the storm of May 26, 1894.

A vicious thunderstorm rattled windows and nerves as it
flashed in the night sky. The bustling mining town and its
more than 400 residents were not used to this kind of storm:

Electrical storms were not unheard of, but they weren't that common, especially storms accompanied by a heavy deluge of rain. As the storm raged overnight, those living upstream along the north fork of Salmon Creek started watching the small creek that ran toward town. The creek was rising steadily.

It was a good thing they were watching. By daylight on May 27, the creek overflowed its banks and began to cut new channels through the middle of town. Debris dams contained most of the overflow upstream until around 8:45 A.M., when, while thunder continued to rumble over the mountains and canyons that fed Salmon Creek, the debris dams broke. A wall of debris-filled water more than 30 feet tall broke loose and started a headlong rush through the narrow canyons toward Conconully. A local resident, Mr. Shufelt, was on horseback in front of Elliott's Hotel when he saw the oncoming flood. He rode through town yelling frantic warnings that gave most of the town's residents enough time to scramble for higher ground before the water hit. But not all were so lucky.

Elderly Mrs. Amelia Keith was staying at her daughter's Conconully home when the family was alerted to the rising water and rushed from the house to escape the flood. Despite the pleading of the family, Mrs. Keith ran back into the house to search for her eyeglasses while the rest of the family watched nearby and hoped that she would get out of the way of the flood in time. Mrs. Keith found her glasses, grabbed them, and was just emerging from the house when the wall of water struck. Though she was just a dozen feet from safety, she was swept away in front of her family members and onlookers. Mrs. Keith was caught in the debris and buried. Although would-be rescuers searched for her, it was not until days later that searchers found her body, and only then with the help of a local dog with a good nose.

The waters continued their rush through town, forcing houses to rise off their foundations and float in the swirling current until the walls collapsed and roofs splashed into the void left behind. As with many towns in the Old West, wood was the primary building material. In Conconully city blocks were raised onto wooden platforms, aproned with plank board-walks. Buildings—bars, general stores, residences—were nailed directly onto these platforms, which led to an unusual situation. One entire city block remained whole and floated as a single unit for 40 feet before it began to disintegrate. Even after the flood, portions of the block remained intact. All told, forty-two buildings fell under the onslaught of the flood—a majority of the buildings in town—and some sections of the town were completely unrecognizable after the flood. A farm and orchard that sat between the town and Conconully Lake, which was downstream on Salmon Creek, was completely transformed and covered by many feet of debris—boulders, trees, and parts of buildings that washed down from the town.

Many narrowly escaped the debris-filled flood. *Glimpses of a Pioneer Life of Okanogan County*—a compilation from the *Okanogan Independent*—tells the story of a Mr. Spence:

He lived far up the creek and had ample time to reach a place of safety but became so dazed that instead of running to the bank not a few yards away, he started down the street in front of the advancing flood. He was caught in the fright-ful war of waters, carried fully a half a mile and deposited in Conconully Lake. An hour afterward someone going to the lake heard cries to help. Spence was clinging to a log.

The last thing that Spence remembered before he found himself in the lake was running into the Schull's Hotel and climbing to the second floor. The water smashed the hotel, and when the flood passed, there was no sign that the building had ever existed.

S. J. Sincock narrowly escaped the flood as well. He was asleep when the water hit his log cabin. He woke when the building collapsed around him, and he rode the floating debris into Conconully Lake, where he emerged without injury.

L. L. Work describes the flood in an article on the Web site "Boom Town Tales & Historic People":

> Along the hill slopes on either side were groups of town folks and the torrent between was filled with floating logs, branches, roofs, scattered house timbers and every imaginable debris. To see such a number of buildings so suddenly endowed with motion, toppling, drifting, collapsing, sinking down to the surface level and floating away as mere wreckage caused a very particular sensation.

Damages from the 1894 flood were estimated at $95,000—no small sum for a small town of the time. In *Told by the Pioneers*, J. Frank Samson recalls notable damage left behind by the flood:

> The lower half of a two-story building was out from under it, leaving the upper half. It still sets where the flood left it. A cement vault, the size of a baker's oven, was the safety place for county records, and was left by the flood in the middle of

an empty lot. A brick and mortar vault for mail also survived the flood and also the fire which later partially destroyed Conconully.

Just as Conconully did following the fire, the town pulled together to rebuild in the wake of the flood. Conconully retained its status as the county seat until 1915, when Okanogan claimed that honor.

CHAPTER 7

"BLACK CLOUD OF DESPAIR"

The Carbonado Mine Explosion

1899

If there is an epicenter for coal mining tragedy in Washington, the tiny town of Carbonado in the foothills of the Cascade Mountains in Pierce County is at the heart of the danger zone. More than one hundred miners have died in accidents since mining started in the mountains around Carbonado in the 1800s.

The morning of December 9, 1899, stands as the most deadly day in Carbonado's history. Shortly after 11 A.M., a huge explosion rocked Carbon Hill Coal Company's Mine Number 7. The *Tacoma Sunday Ledger* described the damage: "The explosion extended to every part of the mine, and the force of it was felt in every gangway, crosscut and shaft from the water level up to almost a thousand feet to the summit of Wingate Hill."

The disaster unfolded in slow motion for those outside the mine. Although Mine Number 7 extended for about 3 miles, including a section that ran underneath much of the town, the

Carbonado Hill Coal Company mine, Carbonado, Washington, ca. 1915.
UNIVERSITY OF WASHINGTON LIBRARIES, SPECIAL COLLECTIONS, UW 5759

explosion happened so far from the town that the townspeople didn't know a disaster was in motion until word was sent down from the entrance to the mine.

Mine officials said the morning shift started normally. Twenty-nine-year-old fireman Rees Jones checked the mine at the start of the shift for unsafe levels of coal gas and dust, but he issued an all-clear, writing "No gas" on a chalkboard at the entrance to the mine, before the miners descended into the darkness. Seventy-six men went down into the mine without any idea that thirty-one of them would not emerge alive.

Rescuers went to work immediately after the explosion, and the outlook was dim for the possibility of survivors. The outlook changed when some miners came out of the still-smoking mine. The *Tacoma Sunday Ledger* described the scene:

There was a dim ray of hope through the black cloud of despair, however, when a party of Hungarian miners appeared from a hill across from the company's office, and in the Czech tongue informed their friends that they had escaped through an old timber air chute from the scene of the accident.

Optimists among the townspeople of Carbonado assumed that this meant that the mining accident would not turn out to be as bad as feared, but it rapidly grew clear over the following hours that the Hungarian miners who escaped were among the minority. Miners who were not on shift at the time of the explosion rushed to the scene and attempted to rescue their cohorts. The majority of the miners rescued were pulled from the tangled timbers in a chute near the summit of Wingate Hill. Many climbed out through the chute or were hoisted up using ropes and ladders from a depth of about 700 feet below the summit. Many survivors were badly burned and blackened by the coal dust and gases that ignited in the explosion.

James Conway survived the initial blast and described the concussion as it hit him and surrounded him with flame. Conway told the *Tacoma Sunday Ledger* that he crawled to a train engine in hopes that the engine would haul him to safety. Other miners scrambled to the engine and together they were hauled out as well.

By 9 P.M., the rescue effort was finished. Mine employees switched to gathering the bodies of the dead and trying to piece together what had caused the blaze. Meanwhile, members of the press tried to get the real story of what happened during the incident, despite mighty efforts by the mine company to limit and control information about the explosion.

To everyone's surprise two survivors were found early in the morning after the explosion. Mike Knish and Peter Merpax were both found in the mine, as the *Tacoma Ledger* reported:

Knish was found groping blindly in one of the workings, uninjured save from slight contact with the damp and the effects of the exposure and fright. Merpax was found unconscious and carried out for dead. He came around upon coming into the open air and asked what time it was. His thought was that he had been asleep and it was time for the shift to come and relieve him. He knew nothing regarding the incident.

It took a few days to determine the cause of the explosion and fire. As was suspected on the day of the fatal explosion, it appeared that the actions of one miner led to the blast. As an article in the *Sunday Tacoma News Ledger* explained: "'So far as well as we can tell,' said Inspector Owens after he came back out of the mine this evening, 'The indications are that the open lamp of Ben Zelder, Sr., caused the explosion.'" The fifty-four-year-old Zelder opened his lamp while inside the mine, in order to light a cigarette. When the open flame from the lamp ignited gas that had built up in the mine, it caused the huge explosion that ripped through the main gangway, from the sixty-sixth chute to the end of the gangway that offered workers access to the mine. The elder Zelder's body was one of the last to be removed from the mine, and next to him an open safety lamp was discovered on the floor of the mine. Zelder died in the explosion, along with his son, whose body was found nearby.

The body of the fireman on duty when the explosion took place, Rees Jones, was recovered near the end of the clean-up process. He was apparently boarding the fourth car of a steam mule train—a steam-powered, small-gauge train used for hauling coal—that was about to head out of the mine at the end of the eight-hour shift when the train was struck by the explosion. Investigators determined that the wreck of this train and the tangle it created in the mine actually helped to save the forty-five men who escaped the blast. The train and the mule that was about to pull it out of the mine when the explosion hit had clogged the mine shaft, allowing the others to escape with little injury.

The Carbonado mine explosion of 1899 was a devastating mining disaster, but it was not the only tragedy or even the most devastating tragedy to strike miners in the state. Five years earlier, on August 24, 1894, a fire in Franklin in King County killed thirty-seven miners when a worker shut down a fan that supplied air to different parts of the mine at the same time that another miner, who was searching for his son, opened a door that changed the mine's airflow. The change in airflow moved smoke from the fire into an area filled with miners, who died of asphyxiation. Sixteen years after the Carbonado tragedy, another coal mine explosion in the foothills of the Cascade Mountains in Ravensdale on November 16, 1915, killed thirty-one miners when an open flame ignited coal dust that had accumulated in the mine.

In the wake of these disasters, and with the decline of railroads and coal-fired steamships for transportation during the twentieth century, coal mining declined in Washington. Oil and natural gas became the resource of choice in the competition for energy dollars. As a result, today the strip-mining operation near Centralia in western Washington ranks as the only major coal mine in operation in the state.

CHAPTER 8

FORTY-TWO DIE ON THE FOURTH

The Tacoma
Trolley Disaster
1900

"Monster Pageant Today in Honor of the Birthday of this Nation," blazed the giant headline on the front page of the July 4, 1900, morning edition of the *Tacoma Daily Ledger*. Stories about the beginning of the Boxer Rebellion in China nestled among articles trumpeting the great celebration taking place in Tacoma. For days Tacoma and Seattle papers had been advertising the massive event. City boosters even ordered special daytime fireworks from Japan—paper birds and animals and a gigantic U.S. flag that would burst from shells launched high into the sky. This was to be no normal Fourth of July.

The battleship *Iowa*, anchored in Commencement Bay, was open for public tours. The state's National Guard regiments filled G Street with an impromptu encampment. Soldiers who fought in the war in the Philippines were meeting for their first postwar reunion, and hundreds of out-of-town visitors, including Governor Rogers and Brigadier General McIntyre, were in town to watch and participate in the big military parade scheduled for 9:30 A.M.

Residents of Parkland, Spanaway, and South Tacoma crowded onto the number 116 trolley car. It was heading downtown under the guidance of F. L. Boehm, an experienced motorman from Cincinnati, and J. D. Calhoun, an inexperienced conductor, who had worked for the Tacoma Railway and Power Company for only two months.

Women and children in their Sunday best made up about half of the one hundred passengers—including Mrs. Lee and her five children, who were heading for the parade. The car was running a little late, but motorman Boehm still took time to check the brakes at the 34th Street stop. The car was so crowded that men were hanging off the car and standing on the running boards. The last boy to be picked up was balanced on the cow catcher at the front of the car.

The car started down the steep hill on Delin Street shortly after 8 A.M. It began to pick up speed and slipped on the rails. Boehm put on the brakes, but the car continued to slip, so he put sand down on the rails to aid traction. The car slowed a bit, but men standing on the running boards acted as if they were going to jump off, feeling that the car was out of control. Boehm told them to stay onboard because he thought he could stop the car at Tacoma Avenue. However, the car picked up speed on the descent and sped past the Tacoma Avenue stop. David Dowden, who was waiting to board at the Tacoma Avenue stop, saw what happened next.

At the base of Delin Street, the tracks curved sharply at 26th and C Streets onto a bridge that spanned a gulch that was more than 100 feet deep. As soon as the car passed Tacoma Avenue, men and boys began jumping from the sides of the car as it careened out of control. The motorman set the brakes hard and put down more sand, but the fuse blew when he reversed the current. None of his efforts were a match for the overloaded car, the steep grade, and the sharp corner at the bridge.

Car 116 did not follow the rails onto the bridge. Instead, it jumped the rails and sailed over the foot-high wood-and-iron guards designed to keep cars on the bridge. Some witnesses later said the car rolled twice in the air before it slammed to the floor of the gulch. People in surrounding blocks heard the crash and immediately ran to the site to see what had happened.

The first at the scene were horrified beyond action by the sight of bodies sprawled down the sides of the gulch and the twist of wood, metal, and flesh 100 feet below the bridge. Charles Hersay, a passenger on another car waiting at the 26th Street switch, ran to a nearby grocery store to call the police. By the time he returned to the side of the bridge, fire engines were responding.

Men and boys who jumped from the car as it sped down the hill were strewn along the road for 300 feet. Some of them survived with scrapes and a few with broken bones. Others were run over and crushed by the car.

While some of the neighborhood residents tended to those on the road and near the top of the gulch, others climbed down banks so steep that the *Tacoma Daily Ledger* noted "that a goat would scarcely be able to descend them." When they reached the wreck, they found dead and dying men, women, and children; dismembered body parts; and misery. They began carrying victims to the top of the gulch in their arms, dragging them on blankets and clothing, or hauling them up with ropes. Some who carried the victims up in their arms later said they had no idea how they did it.

Some of the rescuers found that it was easier to carry the victims 30 feet down to the bottom of the gulch and along the creek that ran there. Boards and logs were placed over the creek, but many were forced to walk in the cold water since that creek bed was flatter and easier to navigate than the steep streamside. Rescuers turned the pump house at the mouth of the gulch into a makeshift hospital and morgue.

Each step or jolt made the injured scream or pass out from pain. At the top of the gulch, the rescuers laid the victims on the grass and then headed back down to find more survivors. Some of the victims died on the trip out of the gulch. Others died soon after. The men and women caring for those at the top covered the faces of the dead with handkerchiefs and clothing, and, along with nurses from Fanny Paddock Hospital, tended the wounds of the living.

One three-year-old boy, nattily dressed in a white shirt and red tie, black pants, navy coat, and a straw hat with a red band, escaped uninjured. The man who rescued him from the side of the gulch took him to the top, gave him a dollar bill, and handed him off to one of the neighborhood women, who took several children into their charge. Since nobody came for him immediately after the accident, the next day's newspaper included a description of him.

When Mrs. Lee was rescued, she found one of her five children, seven-year-old Lyman, who was injured, but not as badly as she was. She was unable to locate her other children, including Richard, Lyman's twin brother. She held Lyman in her arms as they rode to Fannie Paddock Hospital.

The scene they left was gruesome—grass covered in blood, ripped clothing stuck in the shrubs lining the hillside, people groaning and crying with pain and grief. Veterans of the Philippines campaign, in town for their reunion, said the wreckage was worse than anything they'd seen in the war. As one reporter wrote in the next day's edition of the *Daily Ledger*, "Now and then a victim would throw back his head, a 'gurgle' would come from his throat and another victim had been added to the growing list of the dead."

At one point a wagon left for the morgue with nine dead onboard. An ambulance designed to carry one person left carrying three. Survivors arrived at the hospitals with injuries ranging from light scrapes and minor lacerations to broken bones, internal injuries, and head trauma. One story tells of a man and his son who were loaded together onto an ambulance. The boy died on the way to the hospital. When the father stepped from the ambulance and realized his son was dead, he collapsed onto his son with grief. He had to be physically removed to the hospital so that his own injuries could be treated.

By 9 A.M. all of the living had been sent to the hospitals—forty to Fanny Paddock and the rest to St. Joseph's. Many of the dead sent to the morgues were unrecognizable except by their clothing. Half of one man's head had been torn away. At one morgue a disembodied arm arrived with an otherwise "complete," but dead, man.

City officials launched an investigation of the accident immediately following the rescue, and as with all disasters, the citizenry let the rumors fly. Some said that the motorman turned the current on rather than shutting it off as he started down the hill. Experienced street car workers claimed that the motorman probably set the brake too hard, which would have made it impossible for the car to make the turn and forced it off the track. Meanwhile, all of the doctors in the city were called upon to assist in the rescue. They and their nurses worked their heroics to save those they could save and to provide what comfort they could to those who they could not.

Mrs. Lee and her son Lyman were joined at Fannie Paddock by her daughter. While there, she learned that her son Roscoe was safe at St. Joseph's. However, her one-year-old was missing, and Richard, Lyman's twin, was found dead at the scene of the accident. Later Mrs. Lee found that a caring family had taken in her baby.

At St. Joseph's, a pitiful drama that played out over the next few days devastated the Dinger family. Mr. and Mrs. Dinger and their three children—Vida, Dorothy, and six-month-old Floyd—had been among those sandwiched onto the trolley. Mrs. Dinger had been holding Floyd on her lap when the trolley jumped the rails. Mother and babe were found far from each other when they were rescued. Mr. Dinger and Dorothy died immediately. Floyd was taken to St. Joseph's Hospital while Mrs. Dinger and young Vida, the only one to escape without severe injury, were taken to Fannie Paddock. All day and all night, Mrs. Dinger cried for her baby through her pain and delirium, while Vida snuggled next to her. Mrs. Dinger seemed unable to comprehend it when a neighbor told her that her husband was dead. On July 6, the nurses at Fannie Paddock told Mrs. Dinger that baby Floyd was unlikely to survive from his head injury. The *Tacoma Daily Ledger* reported that she "quietly stated, 'If the child's brain will be affected if it should recover, I would rather see it die than live to become an imbecile. I think that would be better for the baby.'" Floyd died later that day, making Mrs. Dinger and young Vida the only survivors of a family of five.

After the accident, the railway company's general superintendent, F. L. Dame, told a *Ledger* reporter that the car was in perfect condition. He did not know how the motorman lost control, but he did say that the rail was bad and the brakes could not hold the train.

In the days that followed, Mayor Louis D. Campbell directed the city to collect money to be dispersed to survivors and those who were widowed and orphaned. Citizens set barrels around town for donations and held fund-raisers. Council members and angry residents blamed the railway for replacing experienced employees with new and inexperienced ones, for overloading its cars, and for allowing them to speed. Ultimately, the city council called upon the state legislature to pass a law ordering performance evaluations of all conductors and motormen.

A coroner's inquest was conducted to determine the cause of the accident. Members of the inquest interviewed the motorman and other survivors, viewed the bodies of the dead, and visited the site of the accident. The brakes on the car were found half set, but nobody paid much attention to that fact since they could have been dislodged when the car hit the bottom of the gulch. However, the investigation revealed that the flanges on the car's wheels were thin and had been unable to hold the car on the rails that themselves were compromised due to more than ten years of use.

The inquest determined that the railway company was at fault for sending Boehm out on a route he had never run before, for improperly maintaining its rails, cars, and the dangerous grade. Several civil suits were filed against the company, and it was almost forced into bankruptcy. The company eventually offered a settlement, and survivors and those widowed or orphaned by the accident split around $100,000—adjusted for inflation, the equivalent of nearly $2 million today.

A YEAR OF FIRES

The Yacolt Burn

1902

W. E. Newhouse knew he was in trouble. The smoke that filled the air, drifting down from the Cascade Mountains, was growing thicker by the minute, and flashes of flames erupted from the smoke as it approached his pioneer home. The mailman had only one choice—to make a mad dash for safety in his mail wagon. Newhouse hitched his horse team and darted down the mountain road at full speed, but the fury of the worst fire in Washington State's history was in hot pursuit. Even with a team of fast horses and a sturdy buggy, the desperate escape attempt failed.

Weeks later, when the smoke cleared, those surveying the fire damage found Newhouse down a gully from the place where a fallen tree blocked his dash from the fire. He was found propped behind a log, huddled against the oncoming flames, with the burned remains of the rattan whip he had been using to drive the horses still in his grasp.

Newhouse was one of more than thirty-eight people known to have died during the fire that became known as the Yacolt Burn. Between September 11 and 13, 1902, the fire consumed everything in its path within a range of 239,000 acres. The southern Washington blaze, hemmed in by Mount St. Helens on the north and the Columbia River on the south, raced toward the tiny town of Yacolt. The flames reached legendary proportions when dry, hot winds from the east pushed the fire 30 miles in thirty-six hours, chasing settlers in its path.

The Yacolt Burn was the largest fire in 1902, a year that was dominated by flames. More than 700,000 acres of forest-land in Washington and Oregon succumbed to the fires that year. At times the skies were so dark with smoke that residents all across western Washington had to carry lanterns to see during the daytime hours.

Like many of the fires started in 1902, no one ever determined the cause of the Yacolt Burn. The possible causes range from lightning strikes to slash burns that flared out of control. Regardless of the causes, a series of fast-moving fires swept out of the mountains and down the river valleys along the North and East Forks of the Lewis River, as well as down the Wind River toward the Columbia River and the site of the present-day town of Trout Lake.

James G. Harris's account of how his family survived the Yacolt Burn in an open meadow on Speelyai Prairie is found in the book *Told by the Pioneers*:

> Many trees fell across the road and blocked the way out. We were hemmed in here and couldn't get out. We sat in our yard with our grips packed from Monday night until Saturday, expecting every day to be burned to death. We lay on the ground most of the time and we kept the babies there all the time, because the only air one could breathe was next

to the ground. The fire went in a semi-circle around this town [Stevenson] or we would have all died.

Similar stories are told of families that survived the fire as it spread toward Trout Lake. More than sixty people survived by building makeshift rafts and floating onto the immense Trout Lake Marsh. They paddled just out of reach of the flames and remained there for two days before the fire died down and allowed them to return to dry land.

Perry Baker also recalled the 1902 fire on the Lewis River in *Told by the Pioneers*:

A pitiful story is told of one mother up on Cedar Creek who took her four children to a cellar cave on the place for protection from the fire. Here they were smothered to death, while less than fifty feet away was a grove of alders about a half acre in extent, which did not burn at all, where they would have been safe.

Frank Barnes, a former senator from Cowlitz County, added his fire tales as well:

The worst fire I remember was in 1902, when 250,000 acres of timber in Clark and Cowlitz Counties burned. Most of this timber belonged to the Weyerhaeuser Timber Company, which had a mill at Yacolt, Washington. The smoke darkened the sun, so that, although we were fully one hundred miles distant, we had to use lights to run our mill and the chickens went to roost in daytime. All day, leaves would come floating through the air and light on the lake. When touched they dissolved into ashes. Many people believed the world was coming to an end. There were many funerals for victims of the fire.

The fire continued its march down the river and creek valleys and closed in on the timber town of Yacolt—due east of Woodland. The townspeople rushed down to the creek side to escape what seemed like impending doom. As they fled the flames, some noticed that the paint on the sides of the buildings was peeling under the approach of the intense heat, even though the fire was still at least a half mile away. The fire rushed right to the edge of Yacolt before shifting winds pushed it north and away from the settlement. Although the townspeople survived, the town was not completely spared from the blaze. As the residents returned to the outskirts of town, they found gruesome scenes. At one farm the pigs that had been held inside their pen along a creek had been cooked alive. The blackened pigs stood where they died, frozen in time by the rushing flames.

The Yacolt Burn drew the attention of Portland and Seattle residents, despite the long distance between the southwestern Washington blaze and the two urban centers. Portland suffered the most direct impact of the Yacolt Burn fires. On one day more than half an inch of ash coated the streets of Portland—with the ash coming from the Yacolt Burn as well as from other fires burning in western Washington and western Oregon. Meanwhile, on the nearby Columbia River, steamboats had to resort to using searchlights to aid their daytime navigation due to the ash-filled skies that turned the day into night.

Aftermath of the Yacolt Burn of 1902.
PHOTO BY RAY M. FILLOON, USDA-FOREST SERVICE

"Seattle Is in No Danger!" declared the *Seattle Daily Times* on September 13, 1902, on a front page that featured drawings of smoke billowing across its banner. With more than seventy fires burning during the dry summer across the Pacific Northwest, Seattle residents were uneasy. When the skies grew dark in the middle of day, the city's residents were sure that the fire had descended from the mountains to the city.

Editions of the *Seattle Daily Times* carried calls for financial aid and stories of the plight of the farmers and woodsmen who had been burned out by the Yacolt Burn. "Comfortable Homes of Well-To-Do Farmers Swept Away by Flames That Claim at Least Forty Lives," declared a front-page headline on September 16, 1902.

"It was on the Lewis River that the fire fiend got in its work of death and destruction," stated an article in the *Seattle Daily Times*. "Beginning near Ariel, a post office some fifteen miles from the mouth of the Lewis River, the flames spread with great rapidity to the foot of Mount St. Helens consuming everything in their path."

The effects of the fires were also noted by ship captains who brought their vessels into ports on the Columbia River, at Grays Harbor, and in Seattle. Captains reported seeing and smelling smoke from the many fires of 1902 as far as 100 miles off the Washington coast.

Although the bulk of damage from the Yacolt Burn happened over a two-day period, fires continued to burn in the area until they were finally extinguished by winter rains and snow. The damage was overwhelming. More than twenty towns were erased by the flames, and at least 158 families were homeless as a result. The fire consumed an estimated twelve billion board feet of timber, and more than one hundred years later, signs of the Yacolt Burn remain visible in the form of burned tree trunks in the areas around Silver Star Mountain on the border between Clark and Skamania Counties.

In the wake of the fire, an icon of the present-day lumber industry sprang to life. The Weyerhaeuser Company, which had been buying forestland to sell to local housing manufacturers who were building the cities of the westward expansion across the country, was the chief beneficiary. For a few years following the conflagration, Weyerhaeuser sent hundreds of

Like many of the fires started in 1902, no one ever determined the cause of the Yacolt Burn.

loggers in to harvest still-standing, burned trees within the boundaries of the Yacolt Burn.

The company notes the historical turn it took following the Yacolt Burn:

> The Yacolt Burn pushed the company into the logging busi-
> ness, and the massive salvage effort helped create friendships
> with local landowners and mill operators. The devastating
> fire also inspired the company to become a leader in public
> and private forest fire protection.

The Yacolt Burn and the vast fires of 1902 also led to a new statewide effort to protect forestlands from similar blazes. In 1903 Washington's state legislature established the office of a state fire warden and a few years later, in 1908, private forest-land owners formed the Washington Fire Protection Association. The jury is still out on how effective fire suppression policies have been over the long run. Many experts are concerned that without the element of natural fires to cut down on the fuels in the forests, the woods are primed for major firestorms.

CHAPTER 10

CURSED AT THE CHRISTENING

The Sinking of the SS *Clallam*

1904

They could see land only 2 miles away. Most of the men onboard chose to sacrifice themselves and loaded all of the women and children, and the ill and elderly, into three lifeboats. A few men joined them in the last boat, which only carried two women. A handful of crew members were charged with guiding the boats to safety. The steamer was taking on water, and the captain believed it would soon rest 150 fathoms below the Strait of Juan de Fuca.

Longtime mariners had predicted a quick and lethal end for the SS *Clallam* when it was launched just ten months before at the Heath shipyard in Tacoma. At the ship's christening, when the bottle of champagne glanced off the prow without breaking and slid down the side of the ship, mariners saw a dangerous omen. When the ensign was unfurled upside down—a universal sign of distress at sea—the fate of the ship appeared sealed. Nevertheless, the Alaska Steamship Company commissioned the steamer and put it to work making the daily run from Tacoma, Washington, to Victoria, British Columbia.

The *Clallam* left Tacoma for Seattle as usual, early in the morning on January 8, 1904. The 168-foot long, 678-ton steamship boasted forty-four staterooms and an 800-horsepower fore-and-aft compound engine and could carry up to 350 passengers. At Seattle the *Clallam* picked up more passengers and freight, including a herd of sheep headed to Victoria for slaughter. Sheep are particularly skittish, and a specially trained bell sheep named Billy was used to lead the others onto ferries. Billy normally cooperated without incident. However, on this morning he behaved strangely and absolutely refused to board for the 8:40 A.M. departure. The boat next headed for Port Townsend before crossing the Strait of Juan de Fuca at noon in a rising gale on a three-hour tour to Victoria.

Capt. George Roberts, a veteran mariner with thirty-two years of experience, was one of the founders of the Alaska Steamship Company and part owner of the *Clallam*. The company had so much confidence in its new steamer that it didn't even have it insured against wreckage, and Roberts was equally confident that its engineer, Scott De Launay, would keep the ship running as it crossed the strait, and, as was his practice, Roberts headed to his cabin for a nap. Near Trial Island, just outside the mouth of Victoria Harbor and about 10 miles from port, De Launay informed Roberts that water was pouring into the hold through a broken porthole. The wind had risen to a full gale and had been buffeting the steamer—which barely reached 13 knots on a good day—in the open water of the strait. Winds on the inner sound were clocked at 36 miles per hour, and on the strait they often blew harder, as high as 50 miles per hour. All the knocking about had also caused the cargo to shift in the boat, leaving it off center. Roberts headed down to find

The SS Clallam was considered a "cursed" ship.
UNIVERSITY OF WASHINGTON LIBRARIES, SPECIAL COLLECTIONS, UW 10684

more than 3 feet of water flooding the engine room. The crew repaired the broken porthole, but water still flowed in. De Launay was unable to locate the leak, but bulkheads contained the water. As later testimony revealed, De Launay did turn on the pumps to empty the hold as the water collected, but that only exacerbated the problem. The pumps began pumping water *in* rather than out. The rising water in the engine room washed coal into the bilge pumps, further inhibiting the crew's efforts to staunch the flow, and by 3 P.M. the rising water killed the fires. The boat was dead in the water. To gain some control of the ship, Roberts ordered the sails raised, and the crew continued to work the manual pumps in the hold.

At 3:30 P.M. the captain consulted with passenger and fellow captain Thomas Lawrence and decided to put the lifeboats over. Women and children were loaded onto the first two boats, along with crew members, and experienced mariners such as Lawrence, who would row the boats to Discovery Island. Some of the women were forced to board lifeboats against their will. One survivor, John Davis, told how he helped forcefully place Jeannie Galletly, who had been injured and was bleeding, into the first lifeboat as she struggled and kicked in an effort to stay onboard the steamer. Charles Bennets, another survivor, told the *Seattle Times* about a man who refused to be left behind. The man tried to jump onboard one of the departing lifeboats, but others restrained him. Nevertheless, the man got away from them and leapt from the side of the *Clallam*. As he flew into the lifeboat, his feet struck one of the women in the face, and he punched right through the bottom of the boat where he became stuck like a cork in a wine bottle. Although at least three survivors recount this story, others remembered no such incident, and it may be apocryphal. Nevertheless, within minutes everyone on the boat perished.

The death of Homer Swaney on the second lifeboat offers an interesting twist for what might have been. Swaney was a wealthy Pennsylvania businessman with rich associates who were backing his Pacific Steel Company, which built blast furnaces at Irondale near Port Townsend and was in the process of establishing a steel plant. Swaney was on track to create a steel-driven metropolis, but his East Coast partners lost interest in the venture when Swaney died.

While Swaney's death may have changed the course of history, one of the most heartbreaking stories of the evening concerns Samuel Bolton and his new wife, who had only been married for ten days and were heading to Victoria at the end of their honeymoon. Bolton placed his wife in the first lifeboat. The boat traveled only a few yards from the steamer before a wave capsized it. Bolton watched in horror until the cold waters claimed his new wife. He then fell to his knees in grief. Fellow passengers restrained him from throwing himself into the stormy seas after his love.

Surviving passenger William King told the *Victoria Daily Colonist* another sad tale of a woman with babe in arms who rode in the second lifeboat.

> After the lifeboat broke, I saw her come up on the crest of a breaker, holding the child high in her arms. I shall never forget the cries of the child. I closed my eyes, and when I looked again they were gone.

King also told the story of Peter La Plant, who watched his wife and child drown. La Plant proclaimed that he no longer had any reason to live and then leapt overboard and drowned. Even after the first two lifeboats capsized, a third boat was loaded with two remaining women, sick or elderly men, and any others who wanted to leave the steamer. Davis and one of the ship's oilers took charge of the boat, but they were unable to find oars and were searching for them when the boat became tangled in the rigging and capsized. Most onboard the lifeboat perished.

The oiler grabbed some wires, and Davis grabbed the oiler's legs, and they both climbed back onto the *Clallam*. They attempted to rescue an elderly man as well, but the old man was unable to hold onto the rope, and Davis saw him sink.

All remaining onboard the *Clallam* tossed freight from the ship to lighten the load and formed bailing crews to forestall sinking. Meanwhile, on Vancouver Island, shortly before 4 P.M., agent Edward Blackwood climbed to the top of the Driard building in Victoria to look for the *Clallam*. He saw the steamer off of Clover Point, just twenty minutes out of port. Blackwood went to Clover Point and confirmed that the steamer was in trouble. He tried to find a tugboat to assist, but none were available in Victoria Harbor, and it would have taken at least five hours for any of the steamers in port to fire their engines and prepare for departure.

Around 5 P.M. Blackwood called Captain Sears of the steamer *Iroquois,* which was at Sydney, and asked him to look for the *Clallam*. It so happened that Sears's brother was a passenger on the steamer. Blackwood also wired Alaska Steamship superintendent Frank Burns in Seattle that the *Clallam* was foundering. Burns sent the Puget Sound Tug Boat Company's *Richard Holyoke* and the *Sea Lion* to search for it. The *Iroquois* searched around Cow Point and as far as Smith Island but was unable to locate the disabled steamer. Sears assumed that the *Clallam* had been found by the other boats so he returned to Victoria around 11 P.M. In the meantime the two tugs searched until around 10 P.M., when the *Holyoke* found the listing *Clallam* halfway between San Juan and Smith Islands. Robert Hall, captain of the *Holyoke*, tied a line onto the *Clallam*. Some stories say that Roberts requested that Hall tow the *Clallam* to Victoria, which was only twenty minutes away, but that Hall decided the prevailing winds would make it easier for the little tug to haul the steamer to Port Townsend. Other stories recall that Roberts asked Hall to tow him to Port Townsend. This fact later became a point of contention during the investigation of the disaster.

Several passengers asked Roberts to place them on the tugboat. Roberts refused and, according to Davis, who was quoted in the January 13 *Seattle Times,* "The captain replied, 'I am running this part of it. When I see we are in danger I will signal for the tug to come back.'" The men onboard continued bailing, and many later said that the sole reason Roberts kept the passengers onboard was so they could help save his ship. However, the added stress of the towline began to pull the *Clallam*'s boards apart, which only served to let more water in. The *Clallam* sank lower and began to list further onto its side. Around 10:30 P.M. the men began screaming and yelling at the tug to turn around, but their shouts went unheard.

The *Clallam* listed and lurched for two more hours, taking hard hits in the stormy strait. Just after 1 A.M. on January 9, when the steamer and the tugboat were midway between Smith Island and Dungeness Lighthouse, the *Sea Lion* arrived. Roberts told its captain that his ship was sinking and asked him to report the fact to Captain Hall on the *Holyoke.* Hall let the line go slack and saw the *Clallam* beginning to capsize. He opened the throttle and sent the *Holyoke* full steam ahead in order to try to right the *Clallam.* For a few seconds the plan seemed to work, but then the steamer failed and listed hard. Hall grabbed an ax and cut the line. The men on the *Clallam* climbed onto the roof of the pilothouse or loaded into the three remaining lifeboats. When the steamer broke apart and started to sink, all were forced into the water, clinging to ladders, doors, and floating in their cork life preservers. The tugboat crews threw lines out and launched lifeboats to haul the victims to safety. Many, however, did not survive, as a story in the *Victoria Daily Colonist* showed, "Three watches found on the [three] bodies had stopped within three minutes of each other showing that the three were drowned about 1:22 A.M."

Bennets was forced into the water and told the *Seattle Times* that he had little hope of surviving. "The water was not cold," he said. "You see we had all been on deck exposed to the wind and rains and the water seemed warm in comparison." Bennets was in the water for only about five minutes when another man pulled him onto a raft. They floated aimlessly for about an hour before the *Sea Lion* pulled the men out and took them, stiff with cold, into the engine room to warm up. The tugboats searched until first light and then returned to Port Townsend with thirty-one survivors. From there, another boat, the *Dirigo*, a ship once captained and sunk by Roberts, took the survivors—twenty-two crew members and nine passengers— to Seattle.

The *Sea Lion* and *Holyoke* headed back to the Strait of Juan de Fuca to search for bodies and possible survivors. Four more tugs also joined the search, partly on the strength of reports that a boat with eight or nine people aboard had survived the waves. The missing lifeboat was never found. Tugboats searched for the bodies of the dead for fifteen days following the sinking. The *Clallam*'s main deck was found on Darcy Island, and bodies surfaced as far away as Esquimalt and Angeles Spit—more than 18 miles from where the ship sank.

Victoria was hard hit by the deaths. Nearly everyone in the city knew at least one of the victims, and many were well-known residents, including the brother of Captain Sears and Jeannie and Jessie Galletly, the daughter and wife respectively of A. C. J. Galletly, manager of the Bank of Montreal, who was sick with grief following the disaster. The death roster and constant funeral and memorial services served to raise the ire of

the residents over these losses. The Victoria Board of Trade
called on Parliament to assist it in an investigation of the accident, but it was determined that the accident involved an
American boat, so the investigation was rightly conducted by
U.S. Marine Inspection Service. Nevertheless, the citizens of
Victoria tried unsuccessfully to secure a warrant for the arrest
of Captain Roberts, and the coroner impaneled a jury for an
inquest. The inquest revealed that one of the lifeboats did not
capsize but sank due to poor maintenance: The ping hole that
lets water out of a landed boat was not capped, and so water
flowed into the boat and caused it to sink. A gruesome article
in the January 12, 1904, edition of the *Victoria Daily Colonist*
told the story:

> The cap, lying in the little dust-marked place which shows
> that it must have lain there for some time, was ten inches or
> more from the open hole. In this boat was the body of Miss
> Harris of Spokane. Seated in the boat, with a lifebelt around
> her, the dead woman's hands clutched the sides firmly and
> her clenched teeth are evident of the grim despair that filled
> her. . . . The position of this body, together with the fact that
> two iron rowlocks, neither of which was attached to the boat
> by any lanyard, and a small gold watch, a lady's small bag
> and a lady's collar were lying to the bottom of the boat,
> showed plainly that it did not capsize.

The investigations in both countries revealed that the
Clallam was fitted with an inadequate rudder and that three
portholes had been broken for at least three months.
Furthermore, they found that the ship carried no distress signals that could have been used to signal passing ships that the

Clallam was in need of assistance, although those who testified offered conflicting accounts on this matter. When De Launay testified in Victoria, he claimed that these facts were largely covered up in the American investigation. The American investigation placed most of the blame on De Launay for not alerting Roberts about the situation in time for him to do anything productive and for not maintaining his equipment. As a result De Launay's license was revoked; Roberts's license was suspended for one year. Also, the jury in Victoria found Roberts guilty of manslaughter, but still placed some blame on De Launay for not properly maintaining the pumps.

Among its recommendations, the Canadian jury suggested that a lighthouse be built on Trial Island. In 1906 the lighthouse was built, and to this day it greets passengers on the ferries that carry tourists from Port Angeles and Seattle to Victoria.

CHAPTER 11

DEATH ON PUGET SOUND

The SS *Dix* Collision
1906

Less than two weeks before Thanksgiving, on Sunday, November 18, 1906, more than seventy passengers loaded onto the SS *Dix*—one of the many passenger ferries of Puget Sound's "Mosquito Fleet"—for the 7 P.M. ferry crossing from Seattle to Port Blakeley. The light breeze and calm sea promised a tranquil forty-minute crossing. Located on Bainbridge Island, Port Blakeley was a bustling mill town and home to what was then the largest lumber mill in the Northwest. Many onboard were returning after a weekend in Seattle spent visiting friends and family or shopping early for their Thanksgiving celebrations.

The clear night provided a pleasant reprieve from the previous week's downpours. The newspapers were filled with reports of the record-breaking floods that were destroying houses and villages across the state. As a result of the floods, debris dotted Puget Sound—raw lumber, large trees complete with tangled root balls, and bits of wood from houses and barns. As the *Dix* left the dock, Capt. Percy Lermond left the bridge to take the passenger fares since there was no purser

The 130-ton and 102.5-foot-long Dix *rolled easily.*
COURTESY OF PUGET SOUND MARITIME HISTORICAL SOCIETY

onboard. Lermond placed the steamer under the control of mate Charles Dennison.

After fifteen-year-old Alice Simpson boarded, she joined the rest of the women and children in the women's cabin. Her longtime friend, Roland Price, and another Port Blakeley resident, John McBane, accompanied her to the cabin. They planned to pass the time chatting until they reached their hometown.

A wooden three-masted steamer, the SS *Jeanie,* under the control of Capt. Philip H. Mason and loaded with iron ore, was about an hour into its journey from Smith Cove to the smelter in Tacoma when the captain and his crew saw the lights of the *Dix* approaching off their port side. Although navigational rules gave the *Jeanie* the right of way, Mason saw no indication that the *Dix* was going to let him pass. Mason watched the *Dix* approach for about five minutes and slowed the *Jeanie* to allow the other boat to pass. However, rather than turning away from the *Jeanie*, the *Dix* drew closer and closer.

Passengers on the deck of the *Dix* saw the other boat's lights closing in on them and heard the crew of the *Jeanie* shouting warnings. When Mason realized that the *Dix* was still on a collision course, he bellowed to Dennison, "Where in the hell are you going?" He then blew the *Jeanie*'s warning whistle three times—the international warning signal of imminent collision from the starboard side. Seemingly oblivious, Dennison kept his course. Mason pulled his boat hard to starboard in order to avoid a straight-on collision. Finally realizing that his boat was in danger, Dennison threw the *Dix*'s engines into reverse. But then, in an inexplicable maneuver, rather than pulling the *Dix* to port a move that could have prevented the collision—Dennison pulled to starboard and straight under the bow of the *Jeanie*. The impact was immediate.

The 130-ton *Dix* measured 102.5 feet and had long been described as difficult to maneuver. Its narrow beam and high cabin made it unstable and caused it to roll easily, especially in choppy seas. At 186 feet and weighing 1,071 tons with a full load, the *Jeanie* dwarfed the *Dix*. The collision rolled the *Dix* into the water on its port side. It righted itself promptly, but not before scooping tons of water into its hold. It began to sink, aft first—and quickly.

McBane, still in the cabin with Simpson and Price, flung open the door of the women's cabin and told the young woman and her friend to get out of the cabin. Price ran out and pulled Simpson after him. The three were immediately washed overboard. McBane and Price both tried to stay near Simpson to ensure that she stayed afloat. Simpson later recalled that McBane's and Price's "only apparent object was to save me."

Men smashed windows in the other cabins and pulled themselves out and into the cold water. Most of those on deck who had not been thrown into the water by the force of the collision jumped overboard. Daniel McEachern, a fourteen-year-old Port Blakeley boy, ran to the bow and with three other men tried to hang onto the lifeboat while the *Dix* sank into the sea. Unfortunately, the lifeboat was tied tight to the stanchions and Daniel was almost sucked down with the boat as the bow sank beneath him.

The bow remained clear of the water for only five minutes after the collision. Few who were in the cabin escaped, and none of the crew below decks survived. Survivors described the horrifying screams and cries of the women and children who remained trapped in the women's cabin and the narrow passage that led from it to the deck. Frank Empie, a Port Blakeley timber inspector who was at the bow when the boats collided, remembered the sounds:

> The screams of women and children reached our ears. These were from the cabin and the little passage way between the side railing and the cabin of the ship. Slowly, the screams died away as the bodies of those who were crying pitifully for help were submerged in the water as the ship began to sink and they were drowned like rats aboard her.

Captain Mason ordered the *Jeanie*'s two lifeboats into the water to save those who had escaped from the *Dix*. He later estimated that he had the boats in the water within ten minutes of the collision. Nevertheless, a handful of the men in the water tried to swim for shore. Sgt. Frey Greyer, a former army swim instructor, swam in the wrong direction. After swimming what he estimated was about a quarter of a mile, he realized his mistake and began swimming back toward the lights of the *Jeanie* and was picked up by a lifeboat. The next day, some longshoremen rescued two Filipino men near Pier 14 in Seattle. The men, Manuel Repeto and Bazzintia Garcia, claimed that they had been aboard the *Dix* and had spent the night swimming the 6 miles from the wreck to shore. Stories of survival like those of the two Filipino men are not unheard of. However, as hypothermia sets in quickly, the average person who is swimming survives only about two hours in fifty-degree water, the approximate water temperature of Puget Sound near Seattle in November.

One man's description of his experience that night perfectly describes the effects of hypothermia:

> For a few minutes, which to me seemed an age, I floated about, going under now and then as a wave struck me. It was not long until my limbs began to get numb. Then I got sleepy and seemed to lose all control of myself. I was half conscious, yet realizing that death was near at hand. Presently I forbot [sic] everything. I seemed to be going down and down. There was no pain nor cold, because I was numb.

He estimated that he was in the water for at least twenty minutes before men in one of the lifeboats picked him up. He was unconscious and floating on a section of railing screen that he'd pulled from the boat as it sank.

Meanwhile, Alice Simpson and Roland Price were some-how separated from John McBane. Although Price could have saved himself by swimming to the *Jeanie*, he insisted on stay-ing with Simpson. She was unable to convince him that rather than dragging her down, her nonabsorbent skirts were in fact helping to keep her afloat. Simpson's billowing skirts luckily trapped air beneath them when she was thrown into the water. The wet fabric became almost airtight and held in air, becom-ing a sort of life preserver. Unfortunately, Price did not survive the ordeal, but Simpson could not say when he drowned since she lost consciousness and did not even remember being saved. McBane, however, did survive with the help of one of the *Dix*'s life preservers, which he and another man hung on to. While floating and waiting for the lifeboats, he saw a third man who was stark naked swimming strongly toward the *Jeanie*. McBane invited him to hang onto the preserver, but the man declined, and as McBane later told reporters, "but he said the *Jeanie* looked better to him. Right straight for her he went, and he was certainly a fine swimmer."

The crew of the *Jeanie* searched for more than two hours and went as far as Whidbey Island, 27 miles from Seattle, look-ing for survivors. Mason and several men who survived said they saw other ships pass the site, and Mason insisted that at least one of them was within hearing distance and should have responded to the distress signal. However, no help arrived and the crew of the *Jeanie* gathered thirty-five survivors, including Captain Lermond and a mate from the *Dix*, before it returned to Seattle. Alice Simpson was the only girl or woman who sur-vived.

Although other boats were dispatched the next morning to look for survivors, none were found. Only one body was recovered, that of Albert McDonald. Mason thought that he recovered all of those who made it out of the cabins and into the water. But, as Alice Simpson could attest, Mason's lifeboats arrived too late to save everyone, including her heroic friend Roland Price. Leonard Masters, a young survivor, could also testify to that fact. Leonard's own father had drowned two years before. On this night the young man was left an orphan—his stepfather drowned and his mother and sister never made it out of the women's cabin.

Port Blakeley sent SS *Florence K* to Seattle to bring survivors home to a dock crowded with people hoping to see their loved ones among the living. Since most of the victims were from Port Blakeley, grief hit the town hard. Ships waiting to be loaded flew their flags at half-mast, and work on the docks was suspended for days following the accident so that the dead could be buried and grieved. While those who knew the victims mourned, others fed their greed. Four days after the accident, the owners of the *Dix*, the Seattle and Alki Point Transportation Company, attempted to sue the owners of the *Jeanie* for $35,000. They claimed that Mason was negligent and ran down the *Dix*.

U.S. marine inspectors Bion B. Whitney and Robert A. Turner headed the investigation that followed. They interviewed survivors, crew, and the captains of both vessels. In the end they placed blame for the incident on Dennison, and they discovered that Dennison did not have a pilot's license and should not have been given control of the *Dix*. They condemned steamship companies in general when they also discovered that it was common practice to not pay for pursers thereby forcing captains to collect fares and leave their boats under the control of crew members. As a result of his negligence, placing the boat in unlicensed hands, Lermond's license was revoked for a year. The *Jeanie* did not escape without blame, however. The investigators found that only one engineer was onboard—at least two were required. They further blamed Captain Mason for not immediately signaling when he saw the *Dix* and for neglecting to fully reverse the *Jeanie*'s engines when collision was imminent.

The *Dix* sank to one hundred fathoms (600 feet) and was never recovered, but not for lack of trying. Because the insurance companies refused to pay without proof of death—meaning a corpse—the U.S. Army Corps of Engineers spent months dragging the bottom until it became obvious that the ship and its victims were irretrievably lost. Although more lives were lost in shipwrecks on the Strait of Juan de Fuca and on the coast, the *Dix* claimed more lives than any other marine accident on the inner waters of Puget Sound.

CHAPTER 12

AVALANCHE!

The Wellington Railway Disaster

1910

Ira Clary, a conductor with the Great Northern Railway, woke with a jolt sometime between 1 and 2 A.M. on March 1, 1910. He realized that the third-class mail car he was sleeping in had been launched from the tracks into the air just before he was tossed repeatedly from the top of the car to the bottom of the car. The tumbling stopped just as abruptly as it began when the car slammed into a tree and wrapped around it, although Clary said it felt as if the car rolled for twenty minutes before it stopped. As Clary described to reporters, the car then "popped open like an eggshell," and he was promptly buried under 6 feet of snow.

Clary was one of eighteen crew members on the Fast Mail Number 27, who, along with the more than sixty passengers and the crew of Spokane Local Number 25 — and at least thirty still-mostly-nameless railway laborers—had been trapped since February 23 in Wellington at the west end of the Cascade Tunnel on Stevens Pass. Both trains were heading west toward the Puget Sound area when massive amounts of snowfall caused small avalanches on both sides of the tunnel. The rails were blocked both east and west.

By most assessments—made in hindsight, of course—the trains should not have been running at all when they started their journey to the west side of the state late in the afternoon on February 22. The whole state had been suffering from extreme weather and heavy snows for most of January and February. The Milwaukee Road and Northern Pacific Railways—whose lines crossed the lower Snoqualmie and Stampede Passes to the south—had determined that the conditions were still too dangerous to send their trains over the mountains.

Even though it was snowing heavily when the trains stopped at Wenatchee and Leavenworth, the last two stops before they began the climb up the east slope, Great Northern superintendent James O'Neill still decided that the trains should attempt the crossing. O'Neill believed that the four rotary plows working the lines could keep the tracks clear, and, as far as he knew, no slides were blocking the route when he gave the go-ahead. However, by the time the trains reached the Cascade Tunnel Station at the eastern entrance to the tunnel, which was 26 miles long, a long slide at Windy Point a few miles west of Wellington was blocking the line, ice was forming on the tracks, and it was snowing even more heavily on the west side of the tunnel. O'Neill realized his error when the train pulling his private car stopped at Wellington. It was then that he learned of the slides to the east, although he did not learn about the slide at Windy Point until the next morning, when he also received news of more slides on both sides of the tunnel.

The trains spent that first night at Cascade Tunnel Station. As O'Neill pondered what should be done, an avalanche came down just behind the two stalled trains and killed two railroad workers who were in a bunkhouse that stood in the path of the snow. O'Neill, in part responding to the demands of nervous passengers that they be moved, was just about to tell the conductor, Purcell, to move his train through the tunnel when he learned that a slide at Wellington blocked the west entrance. As a result, the trains spent a second night at Cascade Tunnel Station.

Just after noon on Thursday, February 24, the trains were sent through the tunnel. Conductor Pettit decided that the trains would be safest about 1 mile west of the tunnel entrance, near Bailets Hotel. The Spokane Local was placed on track four, the one closest to the ledge above Tye Creek. Windy Mountain rose steeply behind the small town and the hotel. Although the slope was steep, up to a 75 percent grade, no avalanches were known to have occurred at that point. However, over the years that the railroad curved around Windy Mountain, logging and fires sparked by trains had denuded the slope. So, when the fateful thunderstorm did strike, no obstacles stood between the cascading snow and the trains sitting at the base of the mountain. Ten miles of slides blocked the trains to the west, and they were soon blocked in from the east as well. The trains were moved just in time, or so everyone thought, when word came on the morning of February 25 that an avalanche had destroyed the cookhouse at the east end of the tunnel, killing two more people and plowing over the exact spot where the trains were parked the day before.

Slides continued almost nonstop over the next couple of days. Some of the slides, which occurred within sight of the trains, took out the telegraph lines on Saturday, February 26, isolating the small town of Wellington. Passengers were nervous about the slides and the constant rumbling that announced even more, but they and the crews made the best of the situation, holding socials and sing-alongs and playing games in the passenger cars before tucking in tight each night.

Although the crews of the rotary plows tried to clear the lines, just as a space was cleared, more snow would slide down to block the lines. Some of the plows were stuck in the slides, and then crews started giving up and hiking to Wellington or down to Scenic, which was 17 miles below and to the west of the tunnel. To make matters worse, the trains were starting to run low on coal, and since the trains had no dining cars or provisions, the food at the bunkhouse and at Bailets Hotel was running out. Passengers grew even more restless. On Sunday a group of railway workers who had not been paid, and who knew that supplies were starting to run low, walked off the job and trekked through the tunnel to Cascade Tunnel Station or down to the Scenic Hot Springs Resort. O'Neill and a crew of railway workers also headed toward Scenic to try to repair the telegraph lines and to get food, supplies, and rescuers up to Wellington to help the stranded passengers to safety at the resort.

The morning of February 28 dawned bright as the light reflected off a landscape of almost solid snow. When the trains had first arrived at Wellington, passengers could see the tops of trees peeking over the snow, but now all was covered. In fact hotel keeper Bailets told passenger John Rogers that the snow was deeper than he had ever seen it. Rogers organized a second group of ten men, including conductor Pettit, and decided to hike the rails to Scenic Hot Springs. Just a short way from

Wellington, an avalanche covered their path and narrowly missed burying one of the men. Pettit decided to turn around and head back to Wellington.

Meanwhile the telegraph lines had been operational for a few hours, and the men who made it to Scenic telegraphed back to Wellington to say that the hike down was not too hard. The message was never received. Just a few letters into the transmission, another slide took the telegraph lines down again. That night, the passengers on the train asked that it be moved back into the tunnel, thinking they would feel safer there, but railway officials were afraid that the trains could get trapped in the tunnel if an avalanche blocked the entrances. And another factor made this option impossible—there wasn't enough coal to move the trains and keep its occupants warm while still ensuring there would be enough for the rotary plows to clear the lines. Some later reports suggest that the train was temporarily moved into the tunnel, but it would have been colder there. And, if fires were burned to keep the passengers warm, they would have risked suffocation.

As much as 8 feet of snow had fallen while the trains were trapped. Warm Chinook winds began blowing, and snow was up to 18 feet deep at Wellington, much of it layered over ice: the perfect conditions for an avalanche.

Very early on the morning of March 1, as many of the train's passengers and railway workers were still settling in for the night, an electrical storm dumped warm rain on the snow that cloaked Windy Mountain so thickly. The thick snow soaked up the water, making it heavy and unstable. The layers of compacted snow covered by ice, then covered by more snow were now heavy with rain. And then—no one report reliably states the time, but it was sometime around 1:45 A.M.—a loud bolt of thunder shook it all loose. The snow slid in one massive sheet—1,000 feet wide and 1,000 feet long—and swept the passenger train, the mail train, and the rotary plow, several electric engines, and the superintendent's private car off the ledge at Wellington and flung them 1,000 feet into the deep gulch that led to Tye Creek. The massive tons of snow that slid down the mountain buried the cars up to 40 feet deep, crushing and suffocating those who otherwise would have escaped without life-ending injuries. W. H. White told reporters that the slide moved slowly and the crackling of trees announced its coming. "Even after the train was struck I had time to think and reason. I closed my eyes and held my breath as the car turned over and over, and wondered what part of my body would get the death blow."

As soon as they realized what happened, Wellington residents and railway workers who had survived the avalanche immediately began to assemble a makeshift hospital at the bunkhouse and began searching for survivors. The exception was Mr. Bailets, who refused to provide sheeting for bandages or winter coats or anything of use to the rescuers. In fact Bailets was walking around his hotel with a gun, threatening anyone who tried to enter. When Basil Sherlock, the telegraph operator, heard about Bailets's behavior, he stomped over to the hotel and berated him. But Bailets refused to assist in any way until Sherlock promised in writing that he would be paid. Mrs. Bailets, with an obviously cooler head and far more empathy, handed over the necessary sheeting.

The few people on the trains who survived and were able, such as Clary, assisted in the rescue attempts. After Clary dug himself out from under 6 feet of snow, he heard Purcell and then saw his hand sticking out of the snow. Clary pulled

Great Northern Railroad crew members and more than sixty
passengers were trapped at the west end of the Cascade Tunnel on
Stevens Pass for more than a week.
UNIVERSITY OF WASHINGTON LIBRARIES, SPECIAL COLLECTIONS, A. CURTIS 17468

Purcell up and dragged him out of the snow. Clary and Purcell
next rescued a fireman named Curly who had been sleeping in
the same car. Clary described what happened next to reporters
from the *Tacoma Daily Tribune*: "The steam from the engine
had melted a big cavern beneath the snow crust, and when
Purcell went to help Curly he fell into this steaming cauldron.
We thought that Purcell would be boiled alive, but we finally
succeeded in getting him out." The trio then headed up the
gully to the bunkhouse. Purcell spent the rest of the night recovering from the ordeal and rolling cotton bandages.

*Removing the first body, that of Sol Cohen, from the avalanche
that killed more than ninety-six people.*
UNIVERSITY OF WASHINGTON LIBRARIES, SPECIAL COLLECTIONS, A. CURTIS 17460

Witnesses told of miraculous survivals and tortuous deaths, including hearing the heart-rending sounds of survivors inside of the cars buried in the snow. Rescuers used anything they could get their hands on to dig. Most of their shovels had been carried down the side of the mountain by the avalanche, so rescuers and survivors alike were digging with their hands. While one woman was found dead with her arms still wrapped around her dead child, another eighteen-month-old baby was found unharmed and "unconcernedly babbling and playfully tossing the snow about," according to Marion Briggs, a Great Northern official who later showed up at the site. Another young child, Raymond Starrett, was traveling with his mother, brother and sister, and grandparents. They were going home after burying Raymond's father, who had been killed by a train. Somebody brought Raymond to Bailets Hotel and left him on the dining-room table, where he writhed with a lacquered wood stick thrust through the skin of his forehead. Sherlock, at the hotel to pick up a couple bottles of whiskey for the bunkhouse-turned-hospital, picked up the child and took him back to the bunkhouse. There he gently cut the stick from the boy's forehead before leaving to search for more survivors. Raymond's mother was later found alive (she spent the rest of her life in a wheelchair). They were the only two surviving family members.

By mid-morning John Wentzel, a railway worker, made it to Scenic to raise the alarm. O'Neill, accompanied by approximately 150 men and a small contingent of nurses, made it back to Wellington at around 1 P.M. He found a total of ten survivors at the makeshift hospital under the ministrations of Mrs. Sherlock and the other dedicated women of the village. Before he left Scenic, O'Neill sent a telegraph message to Everett and told what he knew. At Everett a train was loaded with two coroners, three nurses, four doctors, provisions, and coffins and was sent as far east as it could get before slides blocked its way.

Rescue and recovery proceeded through the day. The would-be rescuers who joined the effort the next day were shocked at the sight. The slope of Windy Mountain was nearly free of snow, the gulch below thick with snow. Except for a few places where wreckage poked through the snow, the scene was almost unremarkable. Those who hiked from Scenic carried heavy packs loaded with food, shovels, and other supplies. The

Seattle Times reported that "the climb is worse than the Chilkoot"—the famed Klondike Gold Rush pass—and it took men two to two-and-one-half hours to walk it.

By the end of the day, as many as 150 men were searching for survivors, and stories and rumors began to make their way to Spokane, Leavenworth, Seattle, Everett, and Tacoma. Over the next week papers reported stories of foreign-workers-turned-rescuers robbing the bodies of the deceased. Many immigrants worked for the railway, including contingents of Japanese men who were brought to the states illegally and specifically to work for Great Northern. In fact at least one car full of immigrant workers tumbled to the bottom of the gulch. Most of the foreign workers who died never made it to Great Northern's official list of the deceased.

Rotary plows were working toward Wellington from both sides of the tunnel, but it would take days before they reached the horrible site. Meanwhile the recovery continued. Some feared that all of the bodies might not be recovered until summer weather melted all of the snow. The dead far outnumbered the surviving and were wrapped in blankets and tied with ropes before being hauled up the steep slope to a temporary morgue in the depot baggage room at Wellington or down to Scenic where a second morgue and makeshift hospital had been set up. Small slides continued to make rescue efforts treacherous. In fact the trainmaster, A. E. Blackburn, was found alive, but as his rescuer was carrying him to safety, another slide hit the pair and killed Blackburn. Of course, as ever with such events, conflicting reports and rumors circulate, and many were never clearly resolved. Blackburn's death is one of these instances. W. J. Manly, another trainmaster, reported that Blackburn had been asleep in the superintendent's car. O'Neill's car moved only a short distance from the track it rested on, but the top of the car was sheered off as if opened with a can opener. Manly said that Blackburn was found inside "as if he had been sleeping peacefully, his face in his hands when the catastrophe occurred."

The scenes that greeted the rescue crew were as violent as those witnessed after the 2004 Indonesian tsunami. Mr. G. H. Davis was found along with his little girl. Both were dead. They were found bound to a tree by iron pipes and rods. An unconfirmed story reported that one man was pulled alive out of the snow after being buried for more than sixty hours; another told of a train car that was excavated and ten people were found alive inside. At other places rescuers dug 20 feet into the snow only to find bloody dismembered limbs and mangled bodies. As bodies started to pile up in the morgues and as survivors grew restless to escape from the ghastly scene, the rescue crews made sleds to carry bodies and people to Scenic.

Eventually, rescue trains made it close to Wellington, and survivors and the dead were carried toward home to Everett and Spokane. The line was not completely clear and operational until March 15, when the first train to Everett carried the rest of the dead, along with any mail that had been found from the mail cars and any personal effects that remained at Wellington. All told, more than ninety-six people died in the avalanche, including thirty-five passengers and at least sixty railroad employees. Only twenty-three people survived, many of them with life-changing injuries.

In 1913 a long concrete shed was built to protect trains from further slides at Wellington. In an attempt to erase the memory of that awful first day of March 1910, Wellington was renamed Tye. Then, in 1929 the 8-mile-long New Cascade

Tunnel was opened and bypassed Tye. But, to this day, travelers who drive U.S. Highway 2 drive through Tye Pass, the site of the horrible disaster. The steep hill down to Scenic from Tye and the steep slope of Windy Mountain make it easy to imagine how difficult the rescue was and how violent the destruction.

CHAPTER 13

THE BIG BLOW

Western Washington Windstorm

1921

Weather forecasters knew there was a storm coming on the morning of January 29, 1921, but even the most seasoned veterans weren't prepared for the gale that would become known as the "Big Blow."

A United States Weather Bureau observer stationed at the North Head Station near the mouth of the Columbia River recalled the sudden rise of the 1921 storm in an official report published in the *Monthly Weather Review*. The unnamed observer reported that after issuing a small craft warning at 8 A.M., he watched the barometric pressure fall rapidly until about 2 P.M., when the pressure seemed to level off. Thinking that the worst of the storm was over with the 24-mile-per-hour winds blowing outside the station, he decided to jump in his car and make a run to nearby Ilwaco for provisions. It was during the return trip to the weather station that the storm suddenly became life threatening.

We proceeded very slowly and with great care, passing over some large limbs that had fallen and through showers of spruce and hemlock twigs and small limbs blown from the trees. We soon came to a telephone pole across the roadway and brought our car to a stop, for a short distance beyond the pole an immense spruce tree lay across the road. We left the machines and started to run down the road toward a space in the forest where the timber was lighter. Just after leaving the car, I chanced to look up and saw a limb sailing through the air toward us; I caught Mrs. Hill by the hand and we ran; an instant later the limb, which was about 12 inches in diameter, crashed where we had stood.

In the hour that the weather observer from southwest Washington had been running errands, the full force of one of the strongest windstorms to hit the Washington coast in recorded history was unleashed. The storm cut a swath along the Oregon and Washington coasts, threatening lives and killing one mill worker in Aberdeen, but the storm's greatest impact was the immense timber damage on the Olympic Peninsula. More than seven billion board feet of timber fell like matchsticks under the onslaught of the wind. In one area near Forks, an entire herd of 200 Roosevelt elk died after being hit by flying tree branches and debris.

When the power of the storm became apparent to the weather observer near North Head on the Columbia River, he ran for his life to find an area devoid of trees. There, he rode out the storm and its winds recorded at more than 100 mph.

The southeast wind roared through the forest, the falling trees crashed to the ground in every direction from where we stood. Many were broken off where their diameter was as much as 4 feet. A giant spruce fell across the roadway burying itself through the planks within 10 feet of where we stood. Three tops broke off and sailed through the air, some of the trees fell with a crash, others toppled over slowly as their roots were torn from the earth. In a few minutes there were but two trees left standing that were dangerous to us and we watched every movement of their large trunks and comparatively small tops.

Weather records from the Big Blow put it solidly among the most intense windstorms in Washington's history. At North Head record keepers clocked sustained winds of 99 mph with an extreme gust of 115 mph. And the effects of the wind spread inland from the coast. Winds gusted to 64 mph in Seattle and 48 mph in Tacoma and Port Angeles. Even far from the storm's path along the coast, in Walla Walla, winds associated with the low-pressure center gusted to 47 mph.

The greatest damage wrought by the 1921 storm hit Clallam County near Forks, where the blowdown of trees hit epic proportions. News reports described tangled wreckage of ancient trees that were felled by the winds. As much as 40 percent of the trees in areas just north of the Hoh River were blown down by the winds, and between 30 and 40 percent of the trees in swaths farther north from Forks were knocked over by the gusts. At the fishing village of La Push, sixteen homes were destroyed by the wind.

Washington historian Murray Morgan noted the impact of the Big Blow of 1921 in his 1955 book, *The Last Wilderness*—including a wind gust of 114 mph and steady winds of 110 mph. "It blew the lighthouse keeper's bull off the island of

Tatoosh, and it bowled over millions of board-feet of old trees in the spruce belt. The giant jack-straw pile of two-hundred-foot-long trees made logging impossible in a wide area on the west end of the peninsula."

Despite the heavy damage caused by the 1921 storm, the low-pressure center at the heart of the storm that caused the Big Blow did not make landfall in Washington, unlike many other large windstorms to hit the coast. In this way the 1921 storm was a small preview of the 1962 Columbus Day Storm that would follow a similar path up the coast before making landfall in Canada.

Following the 1921 storm, it was obvious that Washington had been lucky to escape with only one death. The storm was arguably the second-strongest gale to hit the state during the twentieth century—second only to the Columbus Day Storm. The only reason that there wasn't a larger loss of life was that the Big Blow hit hardest along a sparsely populated coastline.

Thirteen years later in 1934, a weaker windstorm visited Washington on October 21, and despite clocking less-severe top winds around 90 mph in Aberdeen and 83 mph in Tacoma and Seattle, the storm killed twenty-one people and injured more than one hundred in the state. The difference between the 1921 storm and the 1934 storm was the track that the low-pressure cell took as it approached the Washington coast. The 1934 storm made landfall near Neah Bay on the far northwestern tip of the coast, and it cut across the Strait of Juan de Fuca to make landfall again in British Columbia. This track caused winds to speed through the Puget Trough on the east side of the Olympic Mountains—between the Olympics and the Cascade Mountains—putting the strongest winds in the most populated part of western Washington.

Stories from the 1934 gale are harrowing, including the sinking of a purse seiner called the *Agnes* in Ballard that killed five fishermen, and the sinking of a number of boats in Seattle when the transpacific passenger ship the SS *President Madison* broke free from its mooring at Pier 41 and rammed into and sank the sternwheeler *Harvester* and damaged a freight ship before damaging a series of smaller boats.

The carnage caused by the 1934 windstorm was detailed in the *Tacoma News Tribune* on October 22, 1934:

> The coast guard cutter *Haida* was racing out of the Sound to go to the *Floridian* [a steamship in trouble at the mouth of the Columbia River], which later, however, fought its way to safety off shore, when it came upon the sinking purse seiner *Agnes*. Two men were sighted dead in the water as the *Haida* approached, and a third, exhausted, let go the rescue ship's line and was lost. Two others had previously been lost, and two were saved.

Many other windstorms hit Washington between the 1934 event and the big Columbus Day Storm in 1962. Large windstorms hit the state roughly once per decade, with smaller local storms hitting much more frequently. But the big regional events are the ones that stick in the collective minds of long-time Washingtonians—that's the reason that events like the Big Blow of 1921 remain major milestones in the state's history . . . until the next big one.

CHAPTER 14

MOCK BATTLE TURNS DEADLY

The Boeing Field Air Disaster

1937

When most people think of Boeing Field they think of the Red Barn—the building where William Boeing built his first airplane—and big jets, such as the Boeing 747. But, about eighteen months after Boeing Plant 2 was built at Boeing Field, the field was the site of a tragic accident.

Twelve-year-old Larry Ames, a student at Dunlap School in Seattle, was looking out the window of his classroom. Aviation was his hobby, and the navy planes circling overhead captivated him more than his lessons. The planes were stationed at the Sand Point Naval Station on the shores of Lake Washington, just northeast of the University of Washington in Seattle—William Boeing flew his first plane near the site of the naval station in 1915. The planes left the station around 9:30 A.M., and it was common for planes from the station to head to Boeing Field for their mock battles. On this particular Wednesday morning, November 3, 1937, Larry Ames was about to see something that he could never forget.

A PM-4 type amphibious bomber, which looks like a large biplane with a rowboat tacked underneath, had been dipping in and out of the clouds at about 3,500 feet. Two Berliner-Joyce OJ-2 pursuit planes took turns diving and "shooting" at the bomber. Instead of bullets the pursuit planes were equipped with gun cameras that took a series of quick-repeat pictures while the machine gun trigger was engaged. The cloudy morning lent a realistic feel to the battle simulation: Clouds interrupted sight lines and obscured the bomber from the pursuit planes just as they kept the bomber crew from keeping its sights on the would-be attackers.

Five men were aboard the bomber, including two who grew up in Washington State. Lt. Henry B. Twohy, the thirty-year-old pilot, was the son of a prominent Spokane banker, an executive of Old National Bank. Twohy had studied at Gonzaga University before he attended and graduated from Annapolis. He was also newly married, and his wife, Gertrude, had planned a celebration for that evening to mark their six-month anniversary. Cadet Kenneth Rhuddy, a former University of Washington track star, was also newly married, although nobody except his family and a few close friends knew about the marriage. Navy regulations prohibited cadets from marrying, but he broke the rules and married his sweetheart, Ann, seven months earlier, just a month before he graduated from Annapolis. Twohy and Rhuddy were joined on the bomber by cadet K. F. Schmidt, twenty-eight; machinist's mate M. McCrodden, thirty-six; and radio operator R. E. Reagan, thirty-three. The day's exercises were a routine part of their efforts to remain battle-ready and prepared to defend their country.

The bomber reached a speed of 90 mph, and the pursuit planes dove at up to 170 mph during their mock attacks. About an hour into the practice, D. R. French, aviation chief machinist's mate of the Nineteenth Squadron and pilot of one of the pursuit planes, pulled his plane up to about 4,800 feet to let thirty-eight-year-old pilot J. D. Goodsell and his observer, seaman W. S. Bowman, take their turn at the bomber in the other pursuit plane.

Nobody can explain exactly what happened next. Little Larry Ames said he saw the pursuit plane, or as he called it, "a smaller plane," clip the wing of the bomber, "the big plane." And then the planes rolled together in the air and came tumbling down. Goodsell and Bowman extracted themselves from their pursuit plane, but the bomber, after a few moments of what appeared to be controlled flight, rolled and dove straight into a cow pasture just south of Boeing Field. The pursuit plane landed about 300 feet south of the bomber.

An already-panicked Goodsell contended with a defective parachute that did not fully open as he fell to earth. He landed hard, almost on top of the wreckage of his own plane, and was tangled in his parachute lines. His observer, Bowman, landed clear of the wreckage.

I. Winkleman, a passing motorist on U.S. Highway 99, which overlooked Boeing Field, stopped his car and ran into the field to help Goodsell untangle himself from his parachute. Other motorists, shocked by the incredible events they'd just witnessed, also stopped and began wandering onto the field. Tacoma resident S. A. Andres heard the wrenching crash and looked up in time to see both planes tumble through the sky and smash into the field. The thundering impact was heard as far away as Georgetown and Beacon Hill, $5\frac{1}{2}$ miles away. Stanley Combs, who was working at an electrical supply company near the field, ran out of his office when he heard the roar of the engines. He emerged in time to see the two airmen with their parachutes open and debris falling to the ground. He also saw the bomber plow into the damp pasture, where he said it "buried itself so deeply it was hard to determine that it was a plane." A bomber full of fuel slamming into the ground would normally explode into flame, but somehow, sometime before impact, Twohy either cut the engines or they stopped on their own.

None of the five men in the bomber escaped. All were found wearing their parachutes and entombed in the wreckage of the plane. Their parachutes were used as makeshift body-bags when the men were removed from the field.

French and his observer, seaman William D. Smith, helplessly watched the disaster below them and then sped off to Sand Point with a report. Within a few minutes of the crash, a crowd of several hundred people, including journalists, other airmen, and local residents, had gathered on and near the field. Police and navy officials roped off the area around the bomber and posted guards by the wreckage of the pursuit plane. Cdr. A. W. Radford, who was responsible for all operations at Sand Point, rushed to the scene, as did William S. Moore, the inspector for the Bureau of Air Commerce, who was responsible for investigating any commercial aviation incidents. Moore, whose office was at Boeing Field, had been driving into the airport when the planes crashed. However, seeing that it was a military matter, Moore did not investigate since the military had already begun its inquiry.

The next day's newspapers carried pictures of the twisted, crumpled, and almost unrecognizable wreckage. Pilot Goodsell told the *Seattle Times:*

Everything was going fine. We were 3,000 or 3,500 feet over the field, right up near the clouds. Then all of a sudden something happened. And it happened so damn fast I don't know what went wrong.

However, Goodsell told the chief deputy coroner, Harlan Callahan, who drove Goodsell and Bowman back to Sand Point, that he was flying the pursuit plane in an inverted position when he saw part of his plane fly past them. His plane rolled in the air a number of times before it rolled, upside down, onto the wing of the bomber. Although other witnesses said it looked like the pursuit plane dived onto the bomber, Goodsell claimed that he was actually pulling out of a dive when what he thought was one of his plane's wings ripped off, causing the plane to begin tumbling.

Goodsell and Bowman spent a mostly sleepless night in the sick bay at Sand Point but suffered little more than shock. They appeared before the Naval Court of Inquiry, which was headed by Commander Radford, the next day, Goodsell appearing in his flight helmet and full flight gear. Bowman told *Seattle Times* reporters, "I can't talk about it. I've been thinking about those boys and no one will ever know what I went through last night." The court of inquiry hoped to use the film from the gun cameras to show what caused the accident, but when the film was developed, they discovered that most of it had been exposed to light in the crash, and none of the remaining photographs were useful. The court met for several days and heard testimony from military and civilian witnesses. Contrary to Bowman's and Goodsell's claims that their wing ripped off, Smith claimed that he saw no structural damage before the accident, and no evidence to support the missing-wing theory was discovered in the wreckage. Additionally, records showed that, per standard procedure, both planes had been inspected before they took off, and they were found to be in perfect condition. In the end the court was unable to reconcile the conflicting descriptions of witnesses and the chain of events relayed by Goodsell and Bowman. And, in an age before a flight recorder—the black box—was even a figment of an engineer's imagination, the court of inquiry sent its report to the secretary of the navy without finding cause.

Although few people remember this tragedy, anybody who drives past Boeing Field on Interstate 5 passes by the spot where the planes hit the ground. The cow pasture is long gone, swallowed by industrial warehouses and the expansion of Boeing Field. Likewise, the Sand Point Naval Station underwent its own metamorphosis. It served the country well through World War II, and its pilots tested many of Boeing's special designs, but in 1991 the station ceased active operation. Portions of the former base now serve as transitional housing for the homeless, and Magnusson Park, which occupies another part of the base, is quickly becoming one of Seattle's favorite places to relax.

CHAPTER 15

GALLOPING GERTIE

The Tacoma Narrows Bridge Collapse

1940

When Tacoma's residents woke up on November 7, 1940, the wind was kicking up the fall leaves, and the air was touched with a winter chill. A storm that was originally forecast to arrive earlier in the week had stalled and then moved onshore with gusty winds up to 30 miles per hour—nothing out of the ordinary for western Washington in November. But there was something different on this morning, and only those who were trying to drive across the new Tacoma Narrows Bridge, which had been affectionately nicknamed "Galloping Gertie," knew that this morning was extraordinary.

The slender Tacoma Narrows Bridge swayed back and forth in the winds. Since the official opening of the new bridge on July 1, 1940, motorists had noticed on most breezy days the bridge deck would rise and fall in the wind. At times drivers lost sight of cars in front of them as the road undulated. This action is what gave the two-lane highway across the third-longest suspension bridge in the world its nickname: The bridge galloped.

On November 7, however, the bridge was doing more than galloping. As the winds accelerated to nearly 40 mph, the movement became so exaggerated that officials in the tollbooths at each end of the bridge decided to close the span. But a few motorists were still crossing the bridge as it was closed.

Two employees of the *Tacoma News Tribune*—Howie Clifford and Leonard Coatsworth—were among the last people on the bridge. Clifford was working in the *Tribune* offices when he received a phone call about the odd behavior of the bridge in the windstorm. He rushed out to the end of Sixth Avenue and started searching for the perfect viewpoint for a photograph, just in case the bridge was going to fail and fall into the Tacoma Narrows some 160 feet below. According to his account in the *Tacoma News Tribune* on November 8, 1940, Clifford started by taking photos from solid ground on the east side of the bridge, but after he had taken a few photos and sent the film back to the newspaper office with a courier, his curiosity got the better of him, and he decided to go out onto the bridge deck.

Meanwhile, Leonard Coatsworth had just started onto the bridge with his car. Coatsworth eyed the bridge carefully before driving onto the deck, and he noted that unlike on other windy days, during this morning's storm the bridge was swaying in an exaggerated and rapid motion. Nevertheless, Coatsworth ventured onto the bridge with a load of gear from his beach home on the Gig Harbor side of the bridge and his family's dog, Tubby. Coatsworth described what happened next in the November 8 edition of the *Tacoma News Tribune:*

> Either just as I reached the towers, or just as I drove past them, the bridge began to sway violently from side to side. This was something new in my experience with the bridge.

Heretofore, the noticeable motion had been up and down and undulating. Before I realized it, the tilt from side to side became so violent that I lost control of the car and thought for a moment that it would leap the high curb and plunge across the sidewalk of the bridge and into the railing.

I jammed on the brakes and got out of the car, only to be thrown onto my face against the curb. I tried to stand and was thrown again. Around me I could hear the concrete cracking.

Coatsworth briefly attempted to get Tubby out of the car, but the dog wouldn't cooperate. In a split-second decision, the *Tacoma News Tribune* staffer decided to scramble for his life to get off the bridge. Over the next few agonizing minutes, he ran, crawled, and scratched his way roughly 500 yards to the shore. The sudden lurches of the bridge sometimes left him running in midair before he was once again slammed back onto the deck. Behind him, his car slid from one side of the roadway to another as the bridge began to swing even more violently. Filmmakers recorded Coatsworth's struggle to get off the bridge before its collapse in one of the most popular disaster video clips now available on the Internet.

In contrast to Coatsworth's life-and-death dash to get off the bridge, Howie Clifford was being drawn out onto the bridge deck. After taking photos from the shore, Clifford noticed someone standing on the bridge deck near the east tower. The temptation to get to that vantage point and to take the photo of a lifetime drew Clifford onto the bridge, but by the time he arrived at the tower, briefly spoke with the other person, and started taking photos, the bridge began bucking even more violently. He turned around to find he was the only

*This film still shows Leonard Coatsworth's car sliding on the
Tacoma Narrows Bridge, before it collapsed, November 7, 1940.*
UNIVERSITY OF WASHINGTON LIBRARIES, SPECIAL COLLECTIONS, UW 21429

person left near the east tower. Clifford tried to take one more photo when he witnessed the bridge begin to fall apart: "Taking another squint into the ground glass I saw the span begin to buckle and break in the center," Clifford said in a *Tacoma News Tribune* article on November 8. "I pressed the camera trigger and started to run."

Just as Coatsworth had been a few minutes earlier, as Clifford ran toward the eastern edge of the bridge, heading for the shore, he was battered and tossed about. And as Clifford ran for his life, the bridge broke apart, sending the center span along with Coatsworth's car and family dog down to the depths of the Tacoma Narrows. Coatsworth recalled the bridge's last moments in a piece for the *News Tribune:*

> Those who stood on the shore and watched the bridge in its death agony still can have no conception of the violence of the movement felt by one out beyond the towers. Safely back at the toll plaza, I saw the bridge in its final collapse and saw my car plunge into the Narrows.
>
> I saw Clark Eldridge, the bridge engineer [who just happened to be in town when the storm struck], his face white as paper. If I feel badly, I thought, how must he feel? And always through the back of my mind ran the thought—why didn't I save my dog.

While Coatsworth and Clifford were escaping from the bridge deck, witnesses watched another figure scrambling to get off the buckling bridge. *Tacoma News Tribune* reporters caught up with the mystery man, Winfield Brown, a twenty-five-year-old freshman from the College of Puget Sound who paid the dime toll to walk out onto the bridge in the windstorm just for the thrill of the ride on Galloping Gertie. Brown told his story to Associated Press staff writer J. B. Beardwood:

> I was certain I wasn't going to make it. Sometimes the bridge tipped right on its side and I could look straight down at the water, 190 feet below me. I thought I was a goner for sure. The wind was howling and the cement was splitting. The light standards were bending and suspender cables cracking. Pieces of concrete, chipped out of the roadbed, would go whistling by.

Howard Clifford running off the Tacoma Narrows Bridge during its collapse.
UNIVERSITY OF WASHINGTON LIBRARIES, SPECIAL COLLECTIONS, UW 20731

Then, Brown ran off the bridge just 30 feet ahead of Coatsworth.

Although there were many close calls during the collapse of Galloping Gertie, no one died in the catastrophic bridge failure. The lone fatality, other than the bridge itself, was Tubby the dog.

News of the bridge collapse quickly spread around the world. The bridge's original bridge designer, Leon Moisseiff, a New York bridge designer who also helped design the Golden Gate Bridge in San Francisco, was widely criticized in the wake of the collapse. Moisseiff's design for the narrow, two-lane road failed to take into account the aerodynamics of the bridge, which led to its destruction. The original plans for the Tacoma Narrows Bridge included 25-foot-tall open stiffening trusses to support the roadway, but Moisseiff suggested using shorter closed trusses that would create a more graceful looking bridge and also save money on construction costs. Washington State road officials accepted Moisseiff's suggestions and had the bridge redesigned with 8-foot-deep closed trusses.

As a precaution to ensure that similar bridges designed by Moisseiff wouldn't meet the same fate, engineers designed modifications to stiffen the bridges, while allowing the wind to pass through the trusses rather than to push against solid trusses like those used on Galloping Gertie. (Moisseiff's mistakes in designing the Tacoma Narrows Bridge brought the end of his career. He died from heart failure three years later.)

Clark Eldridge, who also drew criticism for the collapse, was dogged by the infamous incident years later. According to the Washington State Department of Transportation, Eldridge was captured by the Japanese during World War II, and while in a prisoner-of-war camp, he was approached by a Japanese officer who had once been a student in America. The officer recognized Eldridge and uttered two words to show his recognition: "Tacoma Bridge."

Local officials pledged to build a replacement bridge as soon as possible after the November 1940 collapse, but the American involvement in World War II delayed completion of a new bridge until October 14, 1950. The new bridge has four lanes—two in each direction—as opposed to the two lanes of the original bridge, and it was constructed with open trusses and stiffening struts that tamed the galloping traits of the first bridge. And today, even though the 1950 version of the bridge

The midsection of the Tacoma Narrows Bridge doing more than "galloping."
UNIVERSITY OF WASHINGTON LIBRARIES, SPECIAL COLLECTIONS, UW 21422

was designed to handle 60,000 vehicles per day, it now carries more than 90,000 vehicles per day—and a twin bridge is being built just to the south of it.

The remains of Galloping Gertie live on underneath the turbulent waters of the Tacoma Narrows. In 1992 the remains of the bridge were placed on the National Registry of Historic Places. Its steel and concrete form an artificial reef that serves as habitat for a wide range of underwater life. The lessons of the downfall of the Tacoma Narrows Bridge are still used in engineering classes around the world.

NOT HOME FOR THE HOLIDAYS

Mount Rainier Plane Crash
1946

Christmas 1946 was just a couple of weeks away. Marine Pvt. Leslie Simmons Jr. was heading home to Kalama, Washington, to surprise his parents. Simmons, a military police officer, had been granted early leave. His father had given him $50 to pay for a bus ticket home, but instead he bought presents with the money and decided to take a seat on one of the six transport planes heading to the Sand Point Naval Station in Seattle from his base in San Diego on December 10. He stuffed his pack with clothes and the gifts, including a formal portrait of himself in dress uniform that he was giving to his mother. Simmons also had good news to share with his family: He'd just been selected to attend officer training school.

Simmons shared his ride home with twenty-eight other marines who had just completed boot camp. Five other planes, also loaded with recruits, formed an aerial caravan for the six-and-a-half-hour flight north. Except for Simmons and the crew, the recruits on this ill-fated plane were there by the luck of the draw—or rather the luck of the alphabet: The soldiers were assigned to planes based on their last names, and this, the last plane, carried the last of the alphabet. Simmons, like most of the other thirty-two marines onboard the Curtiss twin-engine R4-D transport, was just eighteen years old. The young men came of age while World War II ravaged Europe and Asia. They came of age watching movie newsreels and reading news stories about the trials and glories of war. Although the war had ended fifteen months before their December journey, there was much left to do in the postwar era, and after surviving boot camp, they were ready for their first assignments. The plane Simmons rode was operated by twenty-nine-year-old Maj. Robert V. Reilly and two crew members. Reilly was an experienced pilot and a special forces commander. He knew how to handle a plane in the worst of conditions after being stationed in Guam during the war and serving as a test pilot.

The six planes left San Diego late in the morning. As they flew north, the weather degraded. The torrential rains and winds that gusted up to 70 miles per hour buffeted the planes so hard that four turned back near the Oregon-Washington border and sought refuge at Portland. At 4:13 P.M., Reilly radioed to the Toledo station in southwest Washington. He reported that ice was forming on the wings and visibility was so poor that he was flying by instruments alone. He asked to climb to 9,000 feet in order to fly above the weather. According to his calculations and his flight plan, he was about 30 miles south of the Toledo station and less than an hour from landing at Sand Point.

Unfortunately, what Reilly did not know was that the fierce winds he'd been flying through since Salem, Oregon, had blown him 63 miles east, far off course, and in direct line with

Throughout the late spring and summer of 1947, hikers climbed the high ridges to search Mount Rainier's twenty-four glaciers for signs of the missing Curtiss twin-engine R4-D transport.

NOAA CENTRAL LIBRARY

the summit of Mount Rainier. Even if the plane had climbed to 9,000 feet as Reilly had requested, it was not high enough to avoid the 14,410-foot-high mountain. Reilly's 4:13 P.M. call was the last time the plane was heard from. Military officials grew alarmed when Reilly did not call in to Everett by 4:30. When the plane did not land as expected shortly after 5:00, they suspected the worst. Their fears were confirmed as the night wore on with no sign of the plane. Still holding out hope, officials planned a rescue operation to begin the next morning.

The morning of December 11 dawned wet, windy, and gloomy in the lowlands, with blizzard-like conditions on the slopes of Mount Rainier. Search planes loaded with doctors from Sand Point and the Coast Guard station at Port Angeles were grounded until 11:30 A.M. by the awful weather. The one plane that took off from Port Angeles was forced by fog and rain to land at Toledo. However, the pilot, Lt. Ralph Osterberg, reported seeing the crash site just south of Toledo. The state patrol had been conducting a ground search since morning, and Osterberg joined the efforts as soon as he landed. The search focused on the Toledo area because during his final call the day before, Reilly reported that he was about 30 miles south of Toledo, and several residents called authorities to say they had heard a plane in the area late the day before. One resident, P. R. Priel, reported hearing a crash at around 6 P.M.

The Toledo search was unavailing, and by the next morning, Coast Guard Lt. Cdr. R. M. Finley redirected the search to focus on the glaciers that cloak Mount Rainier. Several people reported hearing the plane on December 10, including Mount Rainier National Park's superintendent John C. Preston, who heard it at Longmire at 4:15 P.M., and a park ranger at Paradise Valley, who was the last to hear it. By tracing the plane's route according to the reports of those who heard it, searchers determined that it was on Nisqually Glacier. Weather again hampered an air search—in fact in the eight days that followed the disappearance, 10 feet of snow fell on the mountain, including a blinding blizzard at Paradise on December 13. Nevertheless, ground crews composed of civilian and military mountaineering experts assembled, ready to search as soon as visibility cleared or to head to the crash site should it be located. The rain, wind, and snow kept a detachment of soldiers from McChord Air Force Base and fifty park rangers from heading up the mountain, and planes at McChord, Sand Point, and Port Angeles were grounded.

Finally, seven days after the plane disappeared, the skies cleared and planes took to the air to search the glaciers for the missing aircraft. A total of eighteen planes took off from McChord Field and Port Angeles Coast Guard Station. The break in the weather also allowed the ground searchers to climb the ridges and get better looks at the ice fields. All of the ground parties returned without sighting the wreckage. However, the aerial search revealed two unidentified objects, one near McClure rocks at around 9,000 feet and the other near Pyramid Peak at 6,900 feet. The army sent a helicopter from March Field in California to take a closer look at the objects.

Then, on December 17, Washington State Patrol sergeant Norman Traylor sighted a fire about 25 miles southeast of Eatonville, Washington. He said it looked as if it was flaring from bursts of fuel. The fire was in a remote area that was nearly impossible to gain access to at that time of year. The state patrol sent a plane to search the site while two separate groups of ground searchers headed toward it, one from the east at Longmire and one from the west at Elbe. Meanwhile, finding no evidence of the plane on Mount Rainier, the military expanded its search to include Mount St. Helens to the south and Snoqualmie Pass to the north.

At this point the searchers seemed to be grasping at straws, and they searched based on any rumor or unusual incident even remotely related to the missing plane. A public relations officer at McChord Field intimated that still, after a week without food in the cold, wet, and freezing weather, anything was possible and that the crew and passengers of the plane may somehow have survived the crash and be holed up somewhere awaiting rescue. None of the many rumors, innuendos, or real leads led to the discovery of the plane, and by Christmas the search was called off until summer, when it was hoped that snowmelt would reveal the wreckage. Army and navy planes headed off on an unavailing search of the Olympic Mountains.

The devastated families of the missing marines offered a $5,000 reward for anybody who located the wreckage. Throughout the late spring and summer, hikers climbed the high ridges to search Mount Rainier's twenty-four glaciers for signs of the missing plane. Small-plane pilots, also seeking the fame that would come with finding the wreck, would frequently fly over the mountain. And, in an interesting footnote, it was during one of these flyovers on June 24, that Kenneth Arnold, a Boise, Idaho, pilot who was flying to Yakima from an appointment in Chehalis, saw nine saucer-shaped, tailless vessels zooming in and out of formation over Mount Rainier. He noted the time that it took the objects to fly between the Mount Rainier and Mount Adams and estimated that they had been flying faster than 1,200 miles per hour. In his excitement he forgot about his search for the wreck and hightailed it to Yakima and then onto Pendleton, Oregon, where he shared his story with the *East Oregonian* newspaper, which wired it to the Associated Press. Soon the story was on the front pages of newspapers across the country, and thus, the modern widespread obsession over UFOs began.

Assistant Chief Park Ranger Bill Butler also took part in this informal search. Butler knew the mountain better than most, and on July 21, he spent yet another of his days off climbing the high ridges to look for the plane. On this particular day he was on Success Cleaver, looking west at the South Tahoma Glacier. Late in the afternoon, through his binoculars he spotted a seat, a piece of the fuselage, and a third, unidentified part of the plane. Butler promptly returned to his station and reported his discovery. The next morning found Butler with navy lieutenant Gordon Stanley in a plane over the glacier trying to relocate the wreckage. The air search proved fruitless, and on the morning of July 23, Butler and fellow rangers Gordon Patterson and Bob Weldon established a base camp at Indian Henry's Hunting Ground. Simmons's parents and the parents of some of the other soldiers also headed to the mountain to be there in case their sons were found.

On the morning of July 24, the rangers were joined by experienced guides who worked for the park service and a team of navy personnel trained in mountaineering. The searchers split into three groups: Butler's group climbed Success Cleaver, another climbed the glacier from 7,500 feet, and the third climbed the glacier from 8,500 feet. Each route was dangerous due to falling rocks, slippery ice, and hidden crevasses able to swallow a person whole. Late in the afternoon, the searchers reached their sad goal and confirmed that the debris strewn across the glacier was indeed that of the missing plane. Their first finds included pages of medical records and parts of a marine's uniform. From what the search party discovered, they guessed that the plane crashed head-on into the 8,000-foot cliff and then violently dropped back onto the glacier, scattering debris over a quarter-mile-wide swath. South Tahoma Glacier is riddled with deep crevasses, some large enough that they could hold an entire plane. Due to the dangerous conditions and steep terrain, none of the experienced climbers thought there was a safe way to retrieve the bulk of the wreckage or the bodies of the dead soldiers. Nevertheless, they set out again the next morning at 5:00 to resume the search for the bodies. They spent the day digging up to 15 feet into the ice but were unable to locate any bodies. Rock slides coursed down the mountain all day long, making the whole endeavor dangerous and difficult. When the men returned to base camp, officials again decided to call off the search due to the extreme and dangerous conditions.

The parents of the missing young soldiers, however, were not happy with this outcome. They insisted that more be done to find the bodies of their sons. Relenting to the parental pressure, the navy again assembled a crew of experts who dodged car-sized boulders that careened down the slope of the glacier while they searched for the dead men. Eventually, the searchers found the decomposing bodies. They extracted eleven of the bodies, but the rest were encased in ice or jammed in the nose of the plane, which was so twisted that removal was impossible. As they watched rocks and boulders fly off the glacier's slopes while they contemplated their next steps, the men knew that trying to remove even one body could end in death to themselves or other would-be searchers. They lined up the eleven bodies they had found and buried them in snow before they headed off the mountain for good, carrying the personal belongings of only a few of the fallen soldiers to be returned to their families.

Some of the parents never came to terms with the fact that their sons would not be recovered. However, Ida Tische, who lost her son Kevin, felt that the mountain was a fitting cemetery. She said, "Since he must lie some place, why not leave him at rest on the mountainside, above the flower-bedecked slopes where the deer graze quietly, and where the towering peak of Mount Rainier is God's own monument to him and his companions?"

This memorial dedicated in Veterans Memorial Park in Enumclaw in 1999 honors the thirty-two Marines killed in a plane crash on December 10, 1946, on the South Tahoma Glacier on Mount Rainier. This is an exact replica of the memorial on Mount Rainier, which is accessible only by foot.
JON FUNFAR, CITY OF ENUMCLAW

Even though their sons' bodies were never recovered, the families offered the much-sought $5,000 reward to Bill Butler, but he refused to gain from the tragedy and the deaths of the thirty-two soldiers. Instead, the families bought him a Swiss watch, and some of the families stayed in touch with Butler and were happy to call him a friend.

On August 24, 1947, family members gathered at a roadside view point on Round Pass and in view of the South Tahoma Glacier to remember their lost sons, brothers, husbands, and fathers and placed a memorial stone, carved with the names of all the soldiers. Today, that memorial is no longer accessible by car, but many hikers who learn of the memorial take a detour to see it. In 1999 a second memorial was established at Veterans Memorial Park in Enumclaw. Family members and others still gather there to remember the time that the marines were forced to leave their own behind.

CHAPTER 17

SHAKE, RATTLE, AND ROLL

The Puget Sound Earthquakes
1949 and 1965

People throughout the Puget Sound area were just heading to lunch when the ground started shaking. Five minutes before noon on April 13, 1949, the earth lurched into motion deep under the ground north of the city of Olympia and sent shock waves across the Pacific Northwest.

The 7.1 earthquake—the third large earthquake of the 1940s and the largest since the arrival of European settlers in the Puget Sound region—awakened residents in the rapidly growing urban core of western Washington to the possibility of shifting ground beneath their feet. Prior to 1949 the popular belief was that earthquakes could shake the region, but they were not likely to do significant damage. That all changed with sixty seconds of violent shaking on April 13.

In Tacoma, just a few miles from the epicenter of the quake, the tragedy of the Olympia earthquake played out at Lowell Elementary School. Eleven-year-old Marvin Klegman was leaving the school building to assume his duties as a school patrolman when the quake struck. He was rushing

from class to his post directing fellow students across a cross-
walk on the street nearby when bricks started falling and the
building started crumbling around him. Klegman and most of
his classmates sprinted from the crumbling school to safety
outside, but Klegman realized that a younger student was still
inside the building. He ran back inside to make sure that six-
year-old Kelcy Allen would make it out of the building. As
Allen vividly recalled in a 2003 interview given to KING-TV:
"Someone shouted to me. I turned around and it was a crossing guard. He said, 'We're not supposed to be in here. We've
got to get out of here.'"

Klegman and Allen ran from the building just as a dormer
over the doorway started to collapse. Klegman saw the bricks
falling and jumped on top of Allen, shielding his body from
the bricks. "I remember bricks falling down," Allen said. "He
said, 'Look out!' He then covered me up, and that was the last
thing I remembered." Klegman, the young crossing guard,
never rose from beneath the rubble. He gave his life to save the
younger student. Today, a statue celebrating Klegman's heroism stands in front the of the elementary school, and the
American Red Cross named an award for heroism after him.

Elsewhere around Puget Sound, similar stories played out.
People died in Aberdeen, Castle Rock, and Centralia. Two people died in Olympia and another died in Seattle, and injuries
were widespread. Heavy damage to brick buildings, which partially collapsed during the shaking, caused most of the
injuries. On the Tacoma Narrows Bridge, which was being
rebuilt following its 1940 collapse, a twenty-three-ton cradle
that held the suspension cables on the east tower of the bridge
toppled from its perch and fell 500 feet, crashing through a
barge at the base of the bridge and injuring two men onboard

the barge. Brick buildings and their facades collapsed onto the sidewalks, cars, and people below during the lunch hour in Olympia, Tacoma, and Seattle. And in areas where the ground was not as solid, such as on the Tacoma tidal flats, entire buildings collapsed under the onslaught of the quake.

Reporting in the *News Tribune* one day after the quake, Herman Hunt wrote about the scene along Pacific Avenue in downtown Tacoma:

> The street was full down Pacific Ave., as far are you could see. Motorists, some of whom hadn't felt the shock, looked puzzled too—but stopped their cars. They had to, for there wasn't any place to go.

The Olympia quake was felt across more than 230,000 square miles in the Pacific Northwest, and people felt the most intense shaking up to 85 miles away from the epicenter of the quake. Residents from as far away as Cape Blanco in Oregon, the Idaho panhandle, and even Montana noticed the earthquake. Eight people died as a result of the earthquake, and the economic damage was estimated at more than $100 million. The worst hit areas included Olympia, where a school, church, and library were condemned as a result, and eight buildings on the state capitol campus were badly damaged. The quake even caused a sandy spit that jutted into Puget Sound north of Olympia to sink into the cold waters, leaving the very tip of the spit sticking above the waterline as a new island in the sound.

Outside of Olympia the damage was more limited. Employees at the Northern Pacific Railroad roundhouse along the Puyallup River in the Tacoma tidal flats were shocked when, after the quake, they observed a geyser of water erupting

Eight people were killed as a result of the April 13, 1949, earthquake, including an eleven-year-old boy, Marvin Klegman, from Lowell School in Tacoma. In this photo, two people look at the site where Klegman died.
TACOMA PUBLIC LIBRARY

from under the ground in an area that had been part of the old riverbed.

According to reports in the *News Tribune,* long cracks about 60 feet to 70 feet long appeared at the edge of the railroad track near the point where the geyser shot into the air. The water continued spouting after the earthquake subsided, and when it stopped, it left deposits of white sand along the edges of the hole in the ground. Similar geysers burst to the surface in Puyallup, where geologists suspected that an underground stream was temporarily rerouted by the earth's movement. The

Puyallup geysers caused more than $30,000 in damage to homes, including Darrell Wilson's house, where the water pressure broke the cement floor of his garage and thrust a slab straight up like a wall when the water burst to the surface.

Across all of western Washington, chimneys collapsed and twisted, plaster cracked, and brick walls crumbled in all types of buildings. Centralia and Chehalis had the most extensive chimney damage, with more than 1,300 damaged in Chehalis and nearly every chimney in town damaged in Centralia. Utility services were interrupted for days, with broken water mains and gas mains. And railroad service was stopped for days as well, while tracks in the Olympia area were realigned.

Despite the extensive damage and loss of life, Puget Sound residents had little idea that they were actually lucky in 1949. The Olympia earthquake was triggered more than 50 kilometers beneath the ground. Earthquakes at that depth cause damage, but the shaking is far less violent than that associated with shallow crustal earthquakes that cause sudden jolts that can result in widespread destruction. Scientists have since discovered earthquake faults that underlie heavily populated areas in Puget Sound, such as the Seattle Fault that runs from the Olympic Peninsula through Bainbridge Island and downtown Seattle. The geologic records indicate that these crustal faults have caused 7.0 and larger earthquakes that are much more shallow and more destructive.

Although there was certainly a feeling of being lucky to be alive after the April 13, 1949, earthquake, the survivors with their now wobbly legs and distrust of the ground they stood on were still in for some surprises in the days after the initial quake. The residents of the Salmon Beach community near Point Defiance Park in Tacoma had the most dramatic reason

A police officer surveys the damage of a car buried in rubble.
Many automobiles were destroyed in Seattle, Tacoma, and Puyallup.
TACOMA PUBLIC LIBRARY

to remain jumpy. Three days after the earthquake, on April 16, an eleven-million-cubic-yard landslide, more than half a mile long, narrowly missed hitting homes in the eclectic waterside community—the slipping ground missed the nearest home by less than 20 yards—as the entire bluff overhanging the Tacoma Narrows let loose and slid into the waters below. The slide was so immense that it caused a tidal wave effect on the Tacoma Narrows, pushing water toward Gig Harbor that then rebounded off the opposite shore and rushed back creating waves up to 8 feet high.

Sixteen years later, on April 29, 1965, Warren Mattson was just starting his Thursday morning shift at a plywood mill on the Tacoma tidal flats when the rumbling started once again. As the ground began shaking, Mattson scrambled to safety. He watched and felt the ground shift under his feet in a wave motion—as if he were standing on a shaking tub of gelatin. He didn't know it at the time, but Mattson was near the epicenter of the largest earthquake to strike the Puget Sound region since 1949.

The 6.5 magnitude earthquake broke loose with an epicenter midway between Seattle and Tacoma, roughly 63 kilometers below Point Robinson on Maury Island. Like the 1949 earthquake, the 1965 quake was felt across a wide area—from Oregon to British Columbia, and across the Cascade Mountains in eastern Washington to Idaho—but damage from the quake was spotty and localized around areas where the soils amplified the shaking to cause more damage to buildings. Seven people died and more than thirty were treated for injuries from the earthquake, which rattled Puget Sound for more than forty-five seconds.

The quake struck at 8:29 A.M., and it did its greatest damage in Seattle, where Adolphus Lewis was the first known fatality—struck by falling bricks on South King Street in Pioneer Square. Two more Seattle residents died inside the Fisher Flouring Mills on Harbor Island on the Seattle tidal flats, when they were struck by falling debris. Four others died from heart attacks that were spurred by the shock of the quake—one in Seattle, one in Tacoma, one in Port Townsend, and one in Olympia. The quake did more than $12.5 million in damages, including a wide range of chimney and masonry damage.

Puget Sound residents were reminded of the potential for earthquakes again in 1995, when a deep 5.0 quake struck in roughly the same location as the 1965 shaker. Despite the frequent reminders of the region's earthquake dangers, as illustrated by the 1949 and 1965 quakes, Puget Sound residents remain vulnerable and largely uninformed about the dangers lurking underfoot.

CHAPTER 18

WASHINGTON'S HURRICANE

The Columbus Day Storm
1962

Washington residents were picking up fallen tree limbs and assessing the damage from a strong fall windstorm on the Columbus Day morning of October 12, 1962. Overnight winds had knocked trees down across power lines and set boats drifting into Commencement Bay in Tacoma, where the fire department made periodic runs to retrieve wayward vessels and boathouses. A story in the morning edition of the *News Tribune* warned that another storm could be on the way, but the simple warning left no clue of what was ahead for residents of the Pacific Northwest.

The *Seattle Times* offered more details in its afternoon edition, which arrived on porches hours before the storm, in an article titled, "Very Dangerous Winds—New Storm Coming":

> A "very dangerous" new storm packing winds up to seventy-five miles an hour was moving up the coast toward Washington today. The Weather Bureau raised whole-gale warnings, calling for winds up to seventy-five miles an hour for the Oregon and Washington coasts and the Strait of Juan de Fuca.

More than forty years after the passing of the Columbus Day Storm, residents who lived through the damaging hurricane-force winds can recall stories of extraordinary escape and survival. Although the storm did its worst damage in Oregon, where wind gusts were estimated to peak at more than 170 miles per hour, by the time the big blow reached southwestern Washington, it was packing wind gusts up to 160 mph—the top wind speed was recorded at a radar installation near the mouth of the Columbia River in Naselle, just before it was destroyed by a gust.

Ray Huff had just finished closing for the day at a tire shop in Longview when the skies turned dark and the wind started to howl. "Cottonwood trees started snapping like matchsticks," Huff recalls. "As we made our drive home, a lot of people had their roofs blown off, and there were shingles all over the place. There were so many obstacles in the road on the way home that a drive that normally took ten minutes took more than thirty minutes."

Richard Stratton was in the third grade in Longview when the storm hit, and he posted his memories of the storm on the Web site for the Vancouver *Columbian:*

> I spent most of the evening by the living room windows with my two sisters and brother watching the four sixty- to eighty-foot fir trees across the street blow down one after another. A small trailer rolled end over end down the street at one point, and our back fence blew down. Sometime during the night my Dad climbed up on the roof and replaced some shingles. Neighbors attending the R. A. Long High School football game that night were in the stands when the big flat roof was blown off over their heads and flipped over into the

practice field behind. Power was off for three days and piles of trees were everywhere.

The October 13 edition of the *News Tribune* offered a glimpse of how the storm appeared when it passed through the grounds of the 1962 World's Fair in Seattle:

> Winds up to eighty-three miles an hour whipped the Seattle World's Fair grounds, forcing the fair to close its doors at 9:15 P.M., five hours ahead of the normal closing time. On the fairgrounds, trees snapped like matchsticks and the wind whistling through the towering Space Needle tripod made a sound like a giant tuning fork.

Ernie Linger lived in Seattle when the storm hit, and he recalled how the storm touched his life:

> We didn't expect the storm to be as much as it was. Silver and big leaf maple tree limbs were cracking in the nearby park. We had friends over and the storm kept getting worse and worse. When our friends decided they should go home, they looked out across the city and saw that all of Phinney Ridge was dark. We still had power. It was the worst windstorm I can remember.

Winds throughout the Puget Sound trough in western Washington ranged from 58 miles per hour at Sea-Tac Airport to 88 miles per hour at McChord Air Force Base near Tacoma and 100 miles per hour in Renton. But the fury of the Columbus Day Storm had its biggest impact in the forestlands of the southern Olympic Peninsula and the Willapa Hills, where entire stands of trees were blown down. More than fifteen billion board feet of timber was blown down as the storm rushed north through California, Oregon, and Washington—an amount greater than the combined annual timber harvest in Washington and Oregon during the early 1960s and enough to build more than 1.2 million family homes.

The human toll from the storm was dramatic as well. Forty-six people were killed in Washington, Oregon, and northern California. Nine of those killed were in Washington. Thirty-eight-year-old Roger Whitman was the lone person killed in King County, and he suffered a fate similar to many others who died in the storm—trees fell onto Whitman's truck as he drove through the howling winds. Others were killed after the storm, when they came into contact with downed power lines. The vast majority of Washingtonians in the path of the storm survived by moving away from the doors and windows of their homes and waiting out the wind.

After two straight nights of damaging storms, the state's residents were ready for a return to normal on October 13, as was reflected on the day after the big blow in the *Seattle Times:* "The storm, spawned by Typhoon Frieda, blew itself out yesterday morning over Western Canada. And the Weather Bureau here, in a moment of inspiration, appended to its forecast, 'No gales. . . . No hurricanes. . . . No typhoons. . . . No nothing.'"

The storm continued to make news more than a week after its passing, as Washington's residents surveyed the damage and western Washington was designated a federal disaster area. The *Seattle Times* summed up the damage: "In Olympia, the State Department of Commerce estimated the storm caused more than $20 million damage in six Western Washington counties. The figures did not include King County."

The "Columbus Day Storm" was the largest U.S. storm of its type to come
from a region outside of the tropics in the twentieth century.
NATIONAL WEATHER SERVICE, PORTLAND

Once the damage was tallied, meteorologists looked back
to determine how the storm formed and grew into such a mon-
strous gale—the largest storm of its type to come from a region
outside of the tropics in the twentieth century. The storm was
spawned when a deep barometric low-pressure system formed
off the coast of northern California, and the remains of

Typhoon Frieda interacted with the same storm formation area that had caused the October 11 windstorm. This new low-pressure system formed on Columbus Day and rushed north along the Pacific coast, with the low-pressure center staying about 50 miles offshore. As the storm moved rapidly to the north, winds whipped inland first in the redwood forestlands of northwestern California and then in the trough between the coastal mountains and the Cascade Mountains in both Oregon and Washington.

The barometer readings from near the storm center set all-time records in Astoria, Oregon, and Hoquiam, Washington. And, although the storm center started to degrade once it moved north of the mouth of the Columbia River, by the time the storm blew itself out in Canada, it had destroyed forests, caused death, and knocked down power lines along a path that stretched nearly 1,000 miles.

The final tally from the Columbus Day Storm was impressive, even when compared with the much more common hurricanes that hit the East Coast and Gulf Coast portions of the United States each year. More than 50,000 homes were destroyed along the path of the storm, and nearly 500,000 were left without power—some for days and even weeks after the storm had passed.

THE BIG BLAST

The Mount St. Helens Eruption
1980

"Vancouver! Vancouver! This is it!"

Those frantic words crackling over a radio were the last words ever heard from thirty-year-old geologist David Johnston. He was stationed at an observation post just 5 miles from Mount St. Helens at 8:32 A.M. on the Sunday morning of May 18, 1980, when the volcano that had rumbled to life just a few months earlier exploded in front of him. Johnston was on Coldwater Ridge when he made his radio call to the headquarters office in Vancouver. A scientist until the very end, Johnston was witness to one of the largest landslides in history, followed by a violent volcanic eruption that hurled rocks and debris at speeds estimated at up to 300 miles per hour. Under the onslaught of the blast, there was nothing else to do than to send the radio transmission.

The world-famous eruption of May 18 started with a 5.1 magnitude earthquake centered a mile underneath the mountain. The quake caused the north side of the volcano, which had been growing like a bulging balloon over the days leading up to the eruption, to collapse toward the northwest, sending 3.7 billion yards of rock, ice, and debris into once-pristine Spirit Lake at the base of the mountain and down the Toutle River Valley. At the same time the pressure that had been building inside the volcano was unleashed like a cork being removed from a shaken bottle of champagne. The explosion released energy equivalent to seven megatons, sending a lateral blast out across the old growth forests and mountainous terrain to the north and northwest of the volcano. The blast caught David Johnston a very short time after the eruption started. Anyone within 5 miles of the northwest part of the volcano—squarely in the path of the landslide and blast—died instantly, and in many cases their bodies, like Johnston's, were never found.

The blast rushed across the landscape, ripping down trees and everything in its path, first with a shock wave and then with a superheated rain of rocks. Anything directly targeted by the blast had no chance to escape. The lateral blast covered 230 square miles as it rampaged over the rugged terrain, reaching up to 17 miles northwest of the crater.

The third element of the eruption sent a towering plume of ash and pumice high into the Sunday morning sky. Within fifteen minutes the plume reached an elevation of 80,000 feet—about twice as high as commercial airplanes fly—and started its spread to the east. The fallout from the plume covered the areas up to 10 miles from the crater with a combination of ash and pumice, coating the same landscape that had just been decimated by the landslide and lateral blast, as well as areas to the east of the volcano.

Meanwhile, the upper reaches of the plume carried ash across eastern Washington and Idaho, where it turned day into

Before the 1980 eruption, Mount St. Helens was one of the most frequently climbed peaks in the Cascade Range, and Spirit Lake was a vacation spot offering hiking, camping, boating, and fishing.
PHOTO BY JIM NIELAND, U.S. FOREST SERVICE, COURTESY USGS/CASCADES VOLCANO OBSERVATORY

night with a thick ashfall that coated the ground with inches of dark powder. Widely viewed video showed cars driving in the middle of the day with their lights on to navigate darkened streets. The ash cloud made its way across United States within three days, eventually making its way around the world.

Fifty-seven people fell victim to the eruption. Many died within the first moments of the landslide and lateral blast, including media star and owner of the Mount St. Helens Lodge, eighty-three-year-old Harry Truman, who in the weeks leading up to the eruption had refused to leave his lodge along the shores of Spirit Lake. Truman fit the definition of crotchety

The eruption of Mount St. Helens sent volcanic ash, steam, water, and debris to a height of 60,000 feet. The mountain lost 1,300 feet of altitude.

USGS PHOTO TAKEN BY AUSTIN POST, COURTESY USGS/CASCADES VOLCANO OBSERVATORY

old codger. He was a well-known mountain resident, but he wasn't known for his hospitality and kindly manner. Instead, he gained his fame from yelling at children who dawdled too long over their selection of ice cream treats and from throwing folks out of his lodge. Truman, however, loved his mountain, and when the call came to evacuate the Red Zone, the area around the volcano that state emergency officials had marked as a high danger area, he refused. When the mountain blew, Truman, his pink Cadillac, and sixteen cats and semi-tame, hand-fed raccoon friends, found themselves right in the path of the landslide.

During the initial moments of the eruption, geologists estimate that the landslide pushed the water from Spirit Lake out of its lakebed, burying the lake and Harry Truman's lodge in deposits that were up to 600 feet deep in places. If Truman was outside when the eruption began, he may have felt a cold mist descending from the mountain for a moment before the rush of debris and the heat of the lateral blast incinerated everything. The water in the lake sloshed up the steep sides of the surrounding ridges and then rushed down near its former location, dragging the shattered skeletons of thousands of trees back into the new Spirit Lake. Many of those trees continue to drift across Spirit Lake more than twenty-five years later, pushed from one end of the lake to the other by the prevailing winds.

Keith and Dorothy Stoffel had front row seats for the eruption. They were circling Mount St. Helens in their private plane early in the morning, and, after making one pass around the mountain, they made one last pass and witnessed the start of the landslide from the air. "The whole thing started to slide," Keith Stoffel said in a talk at the Mount St. Helens Visitor

Center at Silver Lake, as reported by the *Oregonian*. "The whole north side of the mountain fell off, basically."

There were many heroes on May 18 and May 19, and helicopter pilot Jess Hagerman was one of them. Hagerman, a National Guard helicopter pilot stationed at Puyallup, was called to fly rescue missions around Mount St. Helens shortly after the eruption began. On the day of the eruption, he rescued the two survivors found closest to the volcano. Jim Scymanky and Leonty Skorohodoff were badly burned by the intense heat of the blast. They had been members of a four-person logging team working near Elk Rock, about 10 miles from the summit of the mountain. In a strange quirk of physics, the sound wave of the blast passed over them, and the ridge they were working near blocked the mountain from their view. They didn't see or hear the eruption, but one of their workmates, Jose Dias, ran around the ridge and yelled in Spanish that the mountain was exploding. No sooner had the words escaped his mouth than the team was blasted by superheated air, ash, and pumice. Scymanky and Skorohodoff stumbled over the ash and pumice to the Toutle River. Hagerman saw footprints in the ash from the air and followed them until he found the men. His crew chief, Randy Famtz, leaped out of the helicopter and into the cement-gray rushing waters of the river to help the two men to a place where Hagerman could land. Both men were badly injured with burns over more than 50 percent of their bodies; Skorohodoff died of his burns ten days after his rescue. Dias was later rescued by someone else, but he died at the hospital, and the fourth member of their crew, Evlanty Sharipoff, climbed a tree and died. His body was not found until fifty-two days after the explosion.

Reid Blackburn's car, located approximately 10 miles from
Mount St. Helens. Reid was a photographer for National Geographic
as well as Vancouver's Columbian newspaper.
USGS PHOTO TAKEN MAY 31, 1980, BY DAN DZURISIN, COURTESY USGS/CASCADES VOLCANO OBSERVATORY

Nobody predicted how extreme the destruction would be if the mountain erupted. Nobody expected it to erupt the way it did, which is one of the reasons that more of the region was not in the Red Zone. Much of southwestern Washington used the mountain and the forests, streams, and lakes around it as their playground—fishing, camping, skiing, and hiking. In fact, just weeks before the blast, Natalie and her parents were skiing across a frozen Spirit Lake. The day before the eruption, the young Moore family—Lu, Mike, and their children, four-year-old Bonnie and three-month-old Terra—headed to the Green River's Valley of the Giants to camp. They felt safe in an area outside the Red Zone, 13 miles, and two peaks away from the mountain. The night of May 17 was quiet and uneventful, and May 18 dawned equally calm and peaceful. But then, as Lu was preparing the family's morning meal, they heard a low rumbling and felt the earth shake and the air grow suddenly heavy around them. Then they saw the roiling clouds of black ash rising over the nearby ridge. Lu began throwing their gear into their backpacks, and the family then sought shelter in an old hunter's cabin near their campsite. When the sky lightened again, they began hiking out of the Valley of the Giants, where most of the trees remained standing, but soon they came to an insurmountable obstacle course of fallen mammoth trees up to 8 feet thick and slick with ash. They headed back toward the valley and, out of water and with their hopes of finding their way out fading, they set up camp, found fresh water, and spent a desolate night in the woods.

The next morning, May 19, the Moore family again tried to hike to safety. A passing helicopter saw them but was unable to land, so a paramedic jumped out to assist the family. Hagerman was back in his helicopter, flying sorties along the Green River in search of survivors and went to help the Moores. With nowhere to set the helicopter down, he lowered it and set part of the landing gear on a fallen tree, then yelled for the Moores to board. As the family loaded into the helicopter, Hagerman and the paramedic yelled at Lu Moore and told her to leave her backpack behind. Lu refused, much to the confusion of the pilot. Hagerman quickly relented when he realized that the Moore's three-month-old baby was inside the pack. Once that was sorted out, the family was lifted to safety.

In the days following the rescue of the Moore family, it grew clear that Hagerman's mission was switching from rescue to the gruesome task of recovering the bodies of those who died in the eruption.

The survival of the Moore family illustrated the random luck that was an important factor in determining who lived and who died in the eruption. It took more than twenty years for many to face the fact that the majority of those who died on May 18, 1980, were killed outside the Red Zone that the state had established around the volcano. Although original news reports and statements from the governor, Dixie Lee Ray, portrayed those who died as reckless thrill seekers who snuck around ROAD CLOSED signs to catch a closer view of the volcano, the truth was that only three of the fifty-seven people killed in the eruption died inside the Red Zone. The majority of those who died were in areas similar to where the Moore family camped—close to the mountain but well outside the boundaries that state officials believed were most at risk for destruction.

The family of Ron and Barbara Seibold was among those who were unlucky and unable to escape the wrath of Mount St. Helens. The whole family, including two children ages seven and nine, where found inside their beat-up car. All four of the Seibolds died when their lungs filled with choking ash.

Trixie Anders was another of those lucky enough to escape the eruption alive. Anders was traveling with a group of geology students, and she made a quick stop for breakfast with her husband while the rest of the group continued toward Mount St. Helens from Randle. According to a story in the *News Tribune*, a friend of Anders, Jim Fitzgerald, continued ahead and was on Spud Mountain, inside the blast zone, where he was able to take fourteen pictures before the blast took his life. Although she never caught up to her original group, Anders

Mailboxes in the mudflow along the Cowlitz River.
USGS PHOTO TAKEN IN JULY 1980 BY LYN TOPINKA, COURTESY USGS/CASCADES VOLCANO OBSERVATORY

was close enough to the volcano to feel jealous at first with the thought that Fitzgerald was getting better pictures from being closer to the eruption, but she soon realized that the group of people traveling in her Jeep was in trouble as well. As she described it to the *News Tribune:*

> We're in a Jeep and driving it so fast, I'm sure we're going to flip it because we went into two corners on two tires. I'm hanging out the back taking pictures, and I said, "OK, if we don't flip the Jeep, the mud's going to get us or the surge is going to get us." I truly did not believe we were going to live.

They survived because the blast ricocheted overhead, deflected by a ridge between their fleeing Jeep and the raging volcano. The story of Anders's escape echoed many others heard in the weeks and years after the eruption. There are many stories of cars flying down Forest Service roads at unspeakable speeds in a race to get away from the eruption, sometimes passing slower vehicles whose occupants did not survive.

Massive amounts of debris, combined with snowmelt and downed trees flooded the Toutle River and all of its tributaries. The river immediately overflowed its banks and swept everything downstream, taking out houses, cars, logging camps, and bridges. The debris rushed to the Cowlitz River and then to the Columbia and eventually the Pacific Ocean. Some who survived the initial blast and sped down the twisting roads were swept away by the river. Summer residents who had cabins along the river watched television broadcasts in horror as they saw their cabins and houses bobbing in the cement-thick deluge that hours before had been a clear-flowing river.

The Mount St. Helens National Volcanic Monument stands in remembrance of those who died and of the destruction that came so quickly. An unnamed ridge near the place where Johnston watched the mountain destroy itself before it took his life was renamed Johnston Ridge. More than a quarter-century later, the eruption of Mount St. Helens remains one of the most universal memories in the Pacific Northwest.

CHAPTER 20

FIRE FROM THE SKY

The Tyee Creek Fire

1994

Residents on the east side of the Cascade Mountains were nervous in the summer of 1994. The summer was unusually dry, and meteorologists predicted a lightning storm—a potent combination that could cause wildfires across the tinder-dry pine and Douglas fir forests and high mountain scrub brush lands.

The fears of lightning-spawned flames turned to reality on Sunday, July 24, when a series of strikes sparked small fires along Tyee Creek and Tyee Ridge, in the heart of the eastern Cascade foothills between Wenatchee and Lake Chelan. The small fires spread slowly at first, held down by a brief temperature inversion that brought high humidity to the area. But after smoldering for a while in the rugged canyons and mountain ridges along the Entiat River, winds whipped the flames together into a solid wall that started marching across the landscape to the north toward the resorts and parks along the shores of Lake Chelan.

Maryann Crossman found herself and her family in the path of the rushing flames on top of Tyee Ridge, and she told a reporter from the *Seattle Times* how her family had only thirty minutes to escape from their home:

> Everybody grabbed and took whatever they thought was valuable. We left with an odd assortment of stuff. We had birds. Somebody grabbed a five-gallon bucket of snap beans we just picked. Someone else pulled all the pictures down off the walls. My grandchildren grabbed everything that looked old, like these kerosene lanterns I use when the power goes out.

Crossman's tale was repeated with variations by more than 400 residents who were evacuated from their homes in the Entiat River Valley in the first days of the Tyee Creek Complex—so named because the fire started many smaller fires that came together in one conflagration. Moments after making her comments to the reporter, she heard from a nearby firefighter that her home had been spared from the flames. But she knew it was too early to rejoice too much. The fire was still on the move.

Most residents in the Entiat River Valley escaped with what they could carry, and days later when they returned to survey the damage, they found little more than smoldering remains of a neighbor's home while right next door the flames had passed by. "It went right around my house," Barry Marsh told the *News Tribune*. "We packed up the pictures, papers and a few cherished items. When it was apparent what was going to happen, my wife took off down the road." Marsh drove away with every belief that his house was gone, but when he returned after the fire had moved on, he found his three-bedroom home standing. The charred path of the flames traced around his green grass yard and flowerbeds. "I was really lucky," Marsh said. "A lot luckier than about a dozen neighbors who don't have homes."

The Tyee Creek fire started small, with roughly 1,000 acres burning on July 25. Newspaper accounts traced the rapid growth of the fire, which doubled in size by July 26. Winds exceeding 30 miles per hour whipped the blaze into an inferno that grew to more than 54,000 acres on July 28. "We had an inversion that held it down for a while," Chelan County sheriff Dan Brelan told a reporter from the *News Tribune*. "But when the inversion lifted, the fire just took off. They've actually had whole trees lift out of the ground, move ahead and start another fire."

At the height of the fire's expansion, it moved a quarter mile every ten minutes. "The wildfire burning in the Entiat River canyon is so vicious that the firefighters are resigned to trying to slow it down rather than stop it," stated an article in the *Seattle Times*. "The spectacular blaze is being stoked by strong winds—many of its own creation—and is racing up and down the forested hills here." At that point the fire had consumed thirteen homes and more than sixty outbuildings, but no one was killed, as homeowners rushed to evacuate in a race to beat the flames.

One day later, on July 29, the Tyee Creek fire nearly reached the southern shores of Lake Chelan just west of the town of Chelan, where vacation cabins and expensive lakeside homes were on the edge of disaster, as the fire exploded in size to scorch more than 70,300 acres. In an effort to save the homes and slow the rapidly growing fire, more than 1,800 firefighters from across the state and around the country descended on the burning landscape. Despite the firefighting efforts the blaze consumed two more homes and fifteen more outbuildings during its rapid upswing, with most of the damage centered in the Entiat River Valley.

On July 30, news accounts stated that the fire had grown to 79,250 acres, and the flames continued to creep closer to expensive homes on the southern shores of Lake Chelan. As 1,000 marines from Camp Pendleton in California geared up to join the fray on the fire lines, emergency officials were busy warning residents to be ready to flee at a moment's notice. The *Seattle Times* spelled out the danger with the help of Al Murphy, the commander in charge of managing the fire response for the Wenatchee National Forest, "'Authorities were prepared to evacuate Chelan if the fire crested the butte,' Murphy said. 'Thick smoke obscured the town and prevented air tankers from dropping retardant on the advancing flames.'" The same article described the efforts that lakeside resident Dee Dee Kronschnabel and her daughter kept up to help save their home:

> Covered in soot and ash, the two had toiled all day as the fire moved closer, filling the air with thick smoke and the smell of burning apples as the flames moved into a nearby orchard. "Too often, people panic and run," said Dee Dee Kronschnabel. "We stayed to try and help by watering our roof and our lawns and cutting away the trees and debris. We hope maybe we can save our house and help save our neighbors' houses."

More than 2,010 people were fighting the Tyee Creek fire by this time, and despite the effort to build a firebreak along 16 miles on the fire's edge, firefighters still had another 26 miles

The Tyee Creek fire consumed 105,960 acres by August 3,
despite the efforts of more than 3,485 firefighters.

PHOTO BY RICHARD UHLHORN

After the Tyee Creek Fire, foresting officials changed their practices,
using prescribed burns and vegetation removal.
PHOTO BY RICHARD UHLHORN

to cover while they hoped for lower winds and rain. Newspapers announced the fire's total damage included 86,000 acres on July 31, as the number of firefighters began splitting time between the Tyee Creek blaze and two other large fires that threatened to do the same kind of damage about 30 miles to the southwest, near Leavenworth.

By August 1, the Tyee Creek fire continued to grow, now to more than 94,290 acres, and to consume a total of nineteen homes, but firefighting officials grew optimistic as they announced the burn was 55 percent contained. "We've got a chance of really containing this thing," U.S. Fish and Wildlife Service spokesperson Laura Pennington told the *Seattle Times*.

"But, we've still got a hot fire and it could get away from us."

Although the fire continued to grow into August 2, the reports remained optimistic. The *Seattle Times* reported that the fire grew to cover 99,270 acres, but the efforts to slow the blaze and to save homes continued to see success.

As the fire wound down, the debate about the root causes of the blaze began to dominate the headlines. One side argued that logging restrictions designed to save habitat for the northern spotted owl led to overgrowth in the forests, and that this overgrowth offered more fuel for the fire, allowing it to grow into the second-largest blaze in Washington's history. On the other hand, another group argued that years of policies aimed at stopping fire in its tracks, and the growing number of Douglas fir trees planted in the area that once supported more sparse and fire-tolerant pine trees, led to the blow up of the big fire.

While the debate raged, the blaze had consumed 105,960 acres by August 3, despite the efforts of more than 3,485 firefighters, and fire-weary residents kept a close eye on the skies for stormy conditions forecasted in local newspapers. The clouds and wind didn't materialize, giving another break to the firefighters.

The *Seattle Times* offered another update on the fire on Saturday, August 16, by which time it had scorched 117,950 acres. Reports showed that the fire was finally 68 percent contained, and firefighters expected to have the fire completely contained four days later. But the march of the fire continued. The Tyee Creek fire didn't stop expanding until thirty-three days after it had been started by lightning, when rain and the efforts of firefighters finally stopped one of Washington's largest forest fires. When the fire was finished, it had covered more than 135,000 acres.

In the aftermath of the second-largest fire in Washington's history, forest management practices were questioned. Fires were frequent summer companions in the Entiat Valley. A 122,000-acre blaze rushed through the picturesque valley in 1970, and 52,000 acres burned in 1988, torching a number of homes. But the Tyee Creek fire seemed different. The U.S. Fish and Wildlife Service determined that the Tyee Creek fire started as a series of small, smoldering fires, and it blew up into a 2,000-acre fire in one day when it encountered an area full of logging slash, where salvage logging had taken place. This analysis served as an argument that one conservation group grabbed to call for a halt to salvage logging and road building. In response the burned timber on private and state forest lands was salvaged, but the debate delayed salvage logging in the burned portions of national forest lands long enough that the charred trees were not harvested.

In an article in *High Country News,* forest recovery manager Tom Graham made these observations:

> If you look at the gross area burned, I'm guessing that easily more than 50 percent was in areas where we've been allowed to manage . . . , but within those areas, some untouched watersheds also burned. The fire was influenced in some cases by past management activities, in other cases not at all.

One year later, in 1995, the Forest Service, the National Park Service, the Bureau of Land Management, and the Fish and Wildlife Service adopted a new National Fire Plan that included increased use of prescribed burns, vegetation removal, and other steps that should be taken to reduce the likelihood of another fire of the intensity of the Tyee Creek burn.

A 6.8 SHAKER

The Nisqually
Earthquake

2001

When the ground started shaking at 10:54 A.M. on February 28, 2001, Puget Sound residents thought they were experiencing the "Big One." The second major earthquake to be unleashed from deep underneath the Nisqually River delta within fifty-two years rolled across western Washington and shook the region for nearly a minute. It was recorded as a 6.8 magnitude quake.

Inside the control tower at SeaTac International Airport, flight controllers struggled to guide planes on approach to the airport as the earthquake began, as described in a story in *The Seattle Times:* "Attention all aircraft in Seattle. We have a huge earthquake going on. The tower is collapsing. I say again: The tower is falling apart. Hang on everybody."

At the same time down on Harbor Island in the Seattle tide flats, U.S. Geological Survey scientist Bob Norris was driving en route to the site of a seismograph on the island to download data and do routine maintenance when his pickup started swaying from side to side. He stopped the truck for a moment, figuring something was wrong with the vehicle, but after stopping he realized he was in the midst of a major earthquake. Norris gunned the engine and drove to a spot where he was clear of any overhead power lines, then he parked the truck and rode out the quake with the rest of western Washington. He had a front-row seat for the largest earthquake in the Puget Sound basin since the 7.1 quake of 1949. Once Norris was parked in what he felt would be a safe area, the real show started. "In less than a second the truck was rocking so violently I lost sight of everything outside and could do nothing but hold on and hope my flying head didn't hit anything," Norris wrote in a narrative for the USGS.

Less than 20 miles away in the Maplewood area near Renton, Paula Vandorssen was on the phone with a friend when she realized what was happening. According to reports in the *Seattle Times,* she screamed into the phone and ran from her living room toward the front door just in time to avoid being swept along with the rear portion of her home toward the Cedar River. She made the right choice. A huge landslide unleashed from the hillside behind her home and rushed down to temporarily dam the river. If she had run to the back door instead of the front, she would have found herself in the midst of the mudslide.

Despite the dramatic damage that simultaneously wrecked buildings across western Washington, the 2001 Nisqually quake was nicknamed by journalists and others, "The Miracle Quake." Why? No one died as a direct result of the earthquake. One death was attributed to the quake—a woman who suffered a heart attack following the shaking died when her husband was unable to reach help by phone. The phone system had stopped working due to the overload of calls right after the earthquake subsided. Given the widespread damage to brick buildings, some of which sent thousands of pounds of bricks flying to the ground below, it was a wonder that no one was buried under all of the rubble.

Western Washington hospitals reported that more than 200 people were treated for injuries caused by the earthquake, but most injuries were minor. Newspapers were full of stories of the fortunate people who narrowly escaped injury or death in the earthquake. In the governor's mansion in Olympia, located just 11 miles from the epicenter, governor Gary Locke's wife, Mona Lee Locke, rushed across the room and plucked her two-year-old son from where he was sitting just moments before a television came crashing down on the spot. Also in Olympia the brick facade on the historic Washington Federal Savings Building collapsed onto the sidewalk. Stan Biles, the city's mayor, was amazed that no one had been seriously injured. As he told the *Seattle Times*: "With each passing hour—and we understand that the amount of damage is even more significant—it is a flat-out miracle that we did not have significant injuries. If this earthquake had happened 90 minutes later, these sidewalks would have been covered with lunchtime pedestrians and recreational walkers."

The most significant damage from the 2001 Nisqually quake was in Olympia, where the northbound lanes of U.S. Highway 101 between Olympia and Shelton had to be closed for repairs of a 120-foot-wide and 30-foot-deep sinkhole that swallowed the roadway. The state capitol building in Olympia also took a beating. The legislature was in session when the quake began, and as legislators and visitors to the capitol climbed out from under desks and doorways when the shaking stopped, they looked up warily at the huge dome on top of the building. The 26,000-metric-ton dome moved nearly 3 inches during the quake and remained in place, and on closer inspection outside the building, there were a number of cracked and twisted columns. The dome was held in place without any fasteners, using gravity alone, which allowed it to shift during the earthquake. In reports following the quake, experts estimated that a large aftershock could have caused the entire dome to collapse, but the aftershock never came.

(Legislators would spend the next two years working in other buildings while repairs were made to the Legislative Building. During those repairs the dome and the structure supporting it were permanently fastened to the rest of the capitol building.)

Damage in Seattle was centralized in the tide flat areas near Pioneer Square, where bricks rained down on the sidewalks and sent pedestrians scrambling for safety. In the headquarters of the Starbucks Coffee Company south of Safeco Field, in the old Sears & Roebuck building that had once held the distinction as the world's largest building by volume, interior portions of the building collapsed, but everyone escaped serious injury. Tales of employees stuck in darkened buildings, fearing for their lives, continue to circulate. And on the Alaskan Way Viaduct, the elevated double-decker highway along the waterfront, cracks were found on the support columns where the roadway had shifted during the earthquake. The damage to the highway, which was known to be an earthquake hazard prior to the 6.8 shaker, was so extensive that city officials immediately began the call for a plan to replace the viaduct. While that call has still not been heeded in the years following the quake, road engineers have stepped in to increase the inspections of the roadway and continue to make temporary repairs to help ensure that the current structure can keep functioning until a long-term plan and funding to replace the roadway are in place.

In Tacoma the hillside above eight homes in the Salmon Beach community near Point Defiance Park was damaged. One house was pushed off the pilings that held it up over the waters of the Tacoma Narrows when a landslide swept down from the oft-moving bluff. (An area nearby had sustained major damage after the 1949 earthquake, and in the interim years, landslides threatened the area during wet winters.)

When the damages from the 2001 earthquake were totaled, experts estimated that the quake caused nearly $1 billion in damage to buildings and roads. As with previous quakes the buildings that sustained the most damage were those that had not yet been retrofitted to more stringent seismic standards, especially those with brick exteriors. And as with the previous major, deep earthquakes in the Puget Sound area in 1949 and 1965, the 2001 earthquake was not followed by strong aftershocks. The depth of the quake was cited by scientists as one reason that there was so little damage in the 2001 Nisqually earthquake

Since the 2001 quake, scientists have revised their estimates for the earthquake dangers in the Puget Sound region. Research has revealed a number of new fault lines, including one that runs under Tacoma, and offered more details about the size of earthquakes that are possible on the Seattle Fault that runs from Bainbridge Island through downtown Seattle toward the east along the route of U.S. Interstate 90. As already proven, the Seattle Fault is capable of producing an earthquake up to a 7.4 magnitude, and since this fault is much shallower than the source of the deep quakes like the 2001 Nisqually earthquake, the stronger ground motion triggered closer to the surface would cause much greater damage— Puget Sound's reminder that it still had not really experienced "The Big One," but it could happen—any day. Luckily for the residents of the Puget Sound region, the last major quake to shake the Seattle Fault happened 1,100 years ago.

CHAPTER 22

MEN, WOMEN, AND FIRE

The Thirtymile Fire

2001

Twenty-one firefighters were dispatched into the woods north of Winthrop in the Okanogan National Forest on July 10, 2001, for what was supposed to be a simple mop-up operation. Little did they know, when they took off after just a couple of hours of sleep, that four of them would not make it through the day alive. A U. S. Forest Service crew of hotshot firefighters designated as Northwest Regulars Number Six was sent in to assess and contain a small twenty-five-acre blaze in rough terrain in the Chewuch River Canyon, near Thirtymile Creek. The fire had been reported by an air tanker that flew over the canyon as it was fighting another fire nearby.

As the firefighters arrived on the scene and started their mop-up work, the fire that had seemed so small from a passing plane erupted into an inferno that put the entire crew in danger. The dry canyon was perfect for a firestorm. Extremely low humidity, an ongoing drought, and temperatures over one hundred degrees were among the conditions the firefighters found when they ventured into the canyon to battle the fire that had started when an inattentive camper left a campfire burning.

Flames race toward firefighting vehicles during the Thirtymile Fire.

Twenty-two-year-old Rebecca Welch, a rookie firefighter working on the second fire of her career, found herself toiling with the rest of the team of firefighters to create a firebreak in an attempt to slow an offshoot of the main fire, when squad leader Tom Craven alerted the crew that they had to leave the area—right now. Craven noticed that the fire conditions were changing and suddenly recognized the danger. The fire was flaring up around them, and their only chance to escape was to make a run for it. Fourteen firefighters beat a fast track away from the fire. Part of the crew loaded into one van and managed to drive out of the area at full speed, but fire blocked the road by the time the second van was loaded. Rather than try to drive through the fire on the road, the remaining crew members in the second van opted to head deeper into the narrow Chewuch River Canyon in search of a safe zone to sit out the fire. The road ahead was a dead end, and the firefighters knew it. They simply didn't have any other option than to drive as far from the flames as possible and find a defensible area to ride out the inferno.

The crew stopped at the end of the road, alongside the small river, with the main fire out of sight over a ridge—the closest thing to a safe area that the firefighters could find. As the fire crested over the ridge and started to march down toward them, the team of fourteen was joined by two panicked hikers—Bruce and Paula Hagermeyer from Thorp—who also were trapped by the flames.

According to Welch's account, as told to the *Yakima Herald-Republic*, the situation took a dramatic turn just after 5 P.M. Welch had been hoping and waiting for the rain that was predicted to fall in the evening, and she started to rejoice when she felt something falling down on and around her. It took Welch only a moment to realize that it wasn't rainfall. Hot embers from the roaring fire rained down from the smoke-darkened sky overhead all around the crew.

Reporter Jesse Hamilton described the scene through Welch's eyes:

> She heard the order to deploy her individual survival struc-
> ture. Carried in a tight package by every Forest Service fire-
> fighter, the single person tents constructed of thin foil-like
> material are used as a last resort. They're designed to ward
> off heat up to 600 degrees. She pulled hers out next to the
> road.

As Welch deployed her fire shelter near the road, the rest of the crew did the same. Because the crew was being pelted by burning embers, there was no time to move to a new location. The crew would ride out the fire wherever they stood when the embers started falling—which meant that Welch would try to survive alongside the road. Others were scattered along the ter-rain at the end of the road into the canyon. Just as Welch started for her shelter, the Hagermeyers ran to her, pleading for help: "They said, 'Help us. Help us. We have to get into your tent.' She let them." They balled themselves up inside and fought to seal the tent's edges to the ground, which is a key to creating a barrier between the unbearable heat of the fire out-side the tent. "All three of us got in it. I don't know how that was possible," Welch said.

While Welch and the Hagermeyers struggled to stay safe under the tiny fire shelter that was built to help a single person survive a fire blowover—the rest of the firefighting crew echoed their actions. Along the road near Welch, seven other shelters were deployed, each filled with one firefighter. In a rocky area above the road, six other firefighters deployed their shelters and struggled to survive the firestorm there.

It is nearly impossible to imagine the heat inside a fire like the one that swept over firefighters during the Thirtymile fire. Fire temperatures in dry eastern Washington fires can climb to between 1,500 and 2,000 degrees—well in excess of the heat shielding capabilities of the shelters deployed by the firefighting crew. Fire shelters reflect roughly 95 percent of the heat from the fire outside the thin tent, and scientists say that humans can withstand temperatures up to 250 degrees for as long as an hour before succumbing to the effects of the heat. Once fire temperatures exceed 500 degrees, the glue that holds a fire shelter together can begin to melt, making the structure even more precarious while the firefighter inside fights for his or her life. "The fire shelter is like a 5 mph bumper on a car," U.S. Forest Service official Dick Mangan told a *Seattle Times* reporter in a July 12, 2001, story. "If you hit that wall at 50 mph, that bumper's not going to help very much."

Yakima resident and crew chief Jason Emhoff was with four other firefighters in a team that was searching for a safe spot to ride out the fire when the embers started raining down. The team started to run toward the river, then deployed the shelters, and as the temperature kept rising inside his shelter, Emhoff decided that he couldn't survive there. He had all of his safety gear, except his heat-resistant gloves, and the heat was just too much as his hands started to cook in the intense hot air. As the fire raged, Emhoff emerged from his shelter and ran toward the road. He crouched behind a boulder for a moment, then ran to a pumper truck to try to survive there. "I just have to think that what saved [Jason's] life was the fact that he didn't have his gloves on," Jason's father, Stephen, told a *Seattle Times* reporter.

Emhoff survived the fire by sheltering inside the truck, but four other firefighters who deployed their shelters nearby were unable to emerge following the inferno. Thirty-year-old Tom Craven, a veteran firefighter who had been leading a squad mopping up a side fire when the inferno began, perished in the blaze along with a trio of less-experienced firefighters— eighteen-year-old Karen Fitzpatrick, twenty-one-year old Devin Weaver, and nineteen-year-old Jessica Johnson. All four of the firefighters deployed their shelters on a rocky rise above the road and the river.

A *Seattle Times* article described what another firefighter, Thomas Taylor, witnessed when he abandoned his fire shelter and ran toward the river:

> Chunks of fire the size of basketballs rained down around him. The heat and smoke were suffocating. Giant walls of flame sounded like waves on a beach, "only 5 million times louder," he told his mother, Gayle Ray. She said Taylor vaulted a forty-inch stump, not sure he would clear it, and stumbled into the water, where he stayed with only his nose poking out for hours.

Of the six firefighters who deployed their shelters on a rocky ledge above the road, only Emhoff and Taylor survived, and they did so by abandoning their shelters when the heat grew too intense. Both ran for their lives, and they barely survived.

As the fire blew over her shelter, Rebecca Welch struggled to tuck herself under the thin protective layer along with the

*Tendrils of fire erupt from the tops of trees as the Thirtymile Fire
takes over a tinder-dry landscape.*

Hagermeyers. "There is no question that she saved us," Bruce Hagermeyer told a reporter. "No doubt about it at all. We would have died." After the fire Dr. Ann Diamond, who treated Welch for the burns on her right side, told the *Seattle Times* that she was sure that the injuries were caused by her efforts to save the Hagermeyers. "It was an heroic act," Diamond told a reporter.

Once the intense heat subsided, the firefighters emerged from their protective shells. The nine survivors gathered on a river bar and stayed together after the worst of the fire had passed. They gathered in a circle to say prayers for those who had died. The survivors made their way out of the fatal burn zone, along with Emhoff, whose hands were burned nearly to the bone, walking away from the scene. They were picked up by rescuers a short time later.

In the wake of the fire—the second most deadly forest fire in state history in terms of loss of life, behind a 1974 fire where five firefighters died when their truck rolled over—the U.S. Forest Service opened an investigation to determine what went wrong and whether firefighters should even have been dispatched to fight the blaze in the first place. The fire started along the edges of Sheep Creek, near the Chewuch River, in an area designated as part of the Chewuch Research Natural Area. One question that remained after the tragic blaze was why firefighters were sent into a designated natural area, when the stated policy was to let the fire burn. Forest Service policy at the time was to fight any fire that started from unnatural means, and since it was known that the Thirtymile fire originated from a campfire that was left smoldering by a careless camper, the firefighters were sent in to clean up the blaze.

The results of the final investigation, announced by the U.S. Forest Service on September 26, 2001, found that a long list of basic firefighting standards were violated throughout the day leading up to the fatal blowup of the fire. "Death and injury were preventable if different actions had been taken through-out the day," said Jim Furnish, the leader of the investigation into the deadly fire, during a press conference. "Almost from beginning to end, the fire potential and fire danger were underestimated."

The results of the Forest Service investigation cited mistakes made by fire managers on the scene, combined with the ongoing drought in the area, low humidity, and weather conditions that provided the perfect trigger for the fire to explode from less than 50 acres to more than 2,500 acres in just hours. One contributing factor may have been the interaction of the fire with a low-pressure weather system that was supposed to bring rain to the fire site on the night of the fire.

The families of the four firefighters who died in the Chewuch River Canyon disputed the Forest Service findings, arguing that they placed too much blame on the victims of the tragic fire.

The long-term impact of the Thirtymile Fire on the U.S. Forest Service was a new focus on firefighter safety and policies that clearly limit firefighting when the dangers are too great. Among the policies that changed in the wake of the fire, the Forest Service pledged to ensure that fire managers and firefighters are fully aware of the developing fire situation, and that they are able to track the fire team's actions in reaction to changing fire conditions.

Family members vowed to make sure that the Forest Service did change its practices after the Thirtymile fire—to guarantee that the same kind of loss of life won't happen again.

Bibliography

WHEN THUNDERBIRD BATTLED WHALE
The Cascadia Subduction Zone Earthquake (1700)

"Earthquake of Enormous Magnitude Hits the Pacific Northwest Coast on January 26, 1700." HistoryLink Web site: historylink .org/essays/output.cfm?file_id=5998.

"The January, 1700 Cascadia Subduction Zone Earthquake and Tsunami," Pacific Northwest Seismograph Network Web site: www.pnsn.org/HAZARDS/CASCADIA/cascadia_event.html.

Seattle Post-Intelligencer. "When Thunderbird Battled Whale, the Earth Shook," March 2, 2001.

"West Coast People Hit by Tsunami," Native American Lore Index Web site: www.ilhawaii.net/~stony/loreindx.html.

GRAVEYARD OF THE PACIFIC
The Columbia River Bar (1841–1936)

Columbia River Bar Information Web site: www.uscg.mil/d13/ units/gruastoria/bar_hazards.htm.

Gibbs, J. A. Jr. *Pacific Graveyard.* Portland, Ore.: Binfords & Mort, 1950.

Grover, D. H. *The Unforgiving Coast: Maritime Disasters of the Pacific Northwest.* Corvallis: Oregon State University Press, 2002.

"USS *Peacock* Wrecks at the Mouth of Columbia River, Giving Her Name to Peacock Spit, on July 18, 1841." HistoryLink Web site: www.historylink.org/essays/output.cfm?file id=5624.

FRESH PAINT HIDES A ROTTEN HULL
The Wreck of the Pacific (1875)

Belyk, R. C. *Great Shipwrecks of the Pacific Coast.* New York: John
    Wiley & Sons, 2001.
"Fragment from Wreck of PACIFIC with Notation by S. P. Moody."
    Vancouver Maritime Museum Web site: www.vancouver
    maritimemuseum.com.
Gibbs, J. A. *Shipwrecks Off Juan De Fuca.* Portland, Ore.: Binfords &
    Mort, Publishers, 1968.
Grover, D. H. *The Unforgiving Coast: Maritime Disasters of the Pacific
    Northwest.* Corvallis: Oregon State University Press, 2002.
Marine Digest. "SS Pacific History," December 28, 1985.
Mason, G. "Ode on the Loss of the Steamship Pacific," Our Roots
    Web site: www.ourroots.ca/e/viewpage.asp?ID=635262.
Wright, E. W., ed. *Lewis & Dryden's Marine History of the Pacific
    Northwest.* The Lewis & Dryden Printing Company, 1895.

A CITY IN FLAMES
The Great Seattle Fire (1889)

Andrews, R. W. *Historic Fires of the West.* Seattle: Superior
    Publishing, 1966.
Newell, G. *The Great Seattle Fire, Totem Tales of Old Seattle.* Seattle:
    Superior Publishing, 1956.
Warren, J. *King County and Its Emerald City: Seattle.* Sun Valley,
    Calif: American Historical Press, 1997.
Works Progress Administration. *Told by the Pioneers,* vol. III.
    Olympia: Washington Pioneer Project, 1938.

A PHOENIX FROM THE ASHES
The Great Spokane Falls Fire (1889)

Andrews, R. W. *Historic Fires of the West.* Seattle: Superior
    Publishing, 1966.
"Ellensburg Fire Destroys 200 Homes and 10 Business Blocks on
    July 4, 1889." HistoryLink Web site: www.historylink.org/
    essays/output.cfm?file_id=5111.
"Fire Destroys 32 Blocks of Spokane Falls on August 4, 1889."
    HistoryLink Web site: www.historylink.org/essays/output
    .cfm?file_id=5131.
Kalez, J. J. *This Town of Ours . . . Spokane.* Spokane, Wash.: Lawton
    Printing, 1973.
Tacoma Ledger. "Northwest Fire Losses Were Big," Tacoma Public
    Library Web site: http://search.tacomapubliclibrary.org/
    unsettling/unsettled.asp?load=Spokane+Fire+of+1889&f
    =disaster\fires.spo.

A WASHINGTON WASHOUT
The Conconully Flood (1894)

Hilderbrand, S. "Flood of 1894 Recalled . . . " *Treasure in the
    Okinagan: Oroville Area History,* vol. 1, 1991.
Okanogan Independent. "Glimpses of Pioneer Life," 1924.
Work, L. L. "1894 Flood in Conconully," Boom Town Tales &
    Historic People Web site: www.ghosttownsusa.com/
    bttales4.htm.
Works Progress Administration. *Told by the Pioneers,* vol. III.
    Olympia: Washington Pioneer Project, 1938.

"BLACK CLOUD OF DESPAIR"
The Carbonado Mine Explosion (1899)

Carbonado Mine Explosion—December 9, 1899. Tacoma, Wash.:
    Pierce County Genealogical Society.
Tacoma Sunday Ledger. "Many Homes Are Made Desolate at
    Carbonado," December 10, 1899.
————. "Thirty-Two Miners Killed," December 10, 1899.

FORTY-TWO DIE ON THE FOURTH
The Tacoma Trolley Disaster (1900)

Hunt. H. "Fourth of July Street Car Disaster," *History of Tacoma*.
    Chicago: S. J. Clarke Publishing Company, 1916.
Seattle Post-Intelligencer. "Coroner's Jury Summoned," July 6, 1900.
————. "Testimony Being Taken," July 12, 1900.
————. "Many Witnesses Called," July 13, 1900.
————. "Examination of Witnesses," July 14, 1900.
Seattle Times. "Tacoma Horror," July 4, 1900.
————. "Jury's Full Verdict," July 16, 1900.
Tacoma Daily Ledger. "Monster Pageant Today in Honor of the
    Birthday of This Nation," July 4, 1900.
————. "List of the Injured Swells the Total Number of Victims to
    over One Hundred, Thrilling Stories of Survivors," July 5, 1900.
————. "Two Score Killed in Street Car Wreck, Frightful Plunge
    over a High Bridge Sends a Happy Fourth of July Crowd into
    Eternity and Saddens Many Homes," July 5, 1900.
————. "Eight More of the Victims of the Wreck May Die at the
    Hospitals. No Hope of Their Recovery Is Entertained by Nurses
    and Physicians," July 6, 1900.
————. "Two More Victims Are Added, Death Record of the Street
    Car Tragedy, Seven of the Injured Are Still Unconscious at the
    Hospitals and Little Hope of Their Recovery Is Entertained,
    More Money Needed," July 7, 1900.

———. "Witnesses Tell of the Wreck," July 12, 1900.

———. "Experts Say the Curve Is Dangerous," July 13, 1900.

———. "Motorman Bohem Did His Full Duty," July 14, 1900.

———. "Jury Scores the Company," July 15, 1900.

A YEAR OF FIRES
The Yacolt Burn (1902)

Carlson, S. "Member Profile: The House That Fredrick Built—The Story of Weyerhaeuser," *Washington Business Magazine,* March/April 2004.

Olson, J. and G. Olson. *Washington Times and Trails.* Grants Pass, Ore.: Windyridge Press, 1970.

Seattle Daily Times. "Seattle Is in No Danger!" September 13, 1902.

Works Progress Administration. *Told by the Pioneers,* vol. III. Olympia: Washington Pioneer Project, 1938.

"Yacolt and the Fire Demon." Clark County, Washington, Web site: www.co.clark.wa.us/aboutcc/proud_past/YacoltBurn.html.

"Yacolt Burn, Largest Forest Fire in Recorded State History, Destroys 238,920 Acres of Timber and Kills 38 People from September 11 to 13, 1902." HistoryLink Web site: www. historylink.org/essays/output.cfm?file_id=5196.

"Yacolt Burn 1902." The *Columbian* archives Web site: www.columbian.com/history/Disasters/yacoltburn.cfm.

CURSED AT THE CHRISTENING
The Sinking of the SS *Clallam* (1904)

Grover, D. H. *The Unforgiving Coast: Maritime Disasters of the Pacific Northwest.* Corvallis: Oregon State University Press, 2002.

Newell, G., ed. *The H. W. McCurdy Marine History of the Pacific Northwest.* Seattle: Superior Publishing Company, 1966.

Seattle Daily Times. "Fifty Lives Lost in Wreck of the Steamer
    Clallam," January 9, 1904.

————. "Conflicting Testimony in Clallam Investigation," January
    19, 1904.

————. "Clallam Sunk by Her Own Pump," January 20, 1904.

Seattle Post-Intelligencer. "Adrift in the Strait," January 9, 1904.

————."Fifty Four Drown in Wreck of the Clallam," January 10,
    1904.

————. "Sea Holds Its Dead," January 12, 1904.

————. "Blame Is Placed on the Chief Engineer," February 14,
    1904.

Tacoma Daily Ledger. "Boy Tells How He Was Saved," January 19,
    1904.

Victoria Daily Colonist. "A Survivor's Story," January 10, 1904.

————. "Captain Roberts' Story of Wreck," January 10, 1904.

————. "Fifty-six Find Watery Graves," January 10, 1904.

————. "Tale of Disaster," January 10, 1904.

————. "A Sad Incident," January 12, 1904.

————. "Michigan Man Says Launching of Boats Was a Terrible
    Error," January 12, 1904.

————. "Scenes Were Turbulent," January 12, 1904.

————. "Capt. Livingstone Thompson Leads a Brigade of Bailers to
    the End," January 13, 1904.

DEATH ON PUGET SOUND
The SS *Dix* Collision (1906)

Newell, G., ed. The *H.W. McCurdy Marine History of the Pacific
    Northwest.* Seattle: Superior Publishing Company, 1966.

Newell, G. and J. Williamson. *Pacific Steamboats: From Sidewheeler to
    Motor Ferry.* Seattle: Superior Publishing Company, 1958.

Seattle Post-Intelligencer. "Boats Find No Trace of Wreck," November 20, 1906.

——. "Finds Life Rafts and Preservers," November 20, 1906.

——. "Dennison Solely to Blame for Wreck," November 21, 1906.

——. "Captain Usually Leaves Pilot House," November 23, 1906.

Seattle Times. "Dix Sinks in Collision; Forty Two Lost," November 19, 1906.

——. "Jeanie's Captain Blames Dix's Helmsman," November 19, 1906.

——. "May Try to Raise Sunken Death Trap," November 19, 1906.

——. "Port Blakely Stricken with Grief," November 19, 1906.

——. "Wreck May Never Be Recovered," November 19, 1906.

Tacoma Daily Ledger, "Steamer Dix Sunk by Jeanie Forty Passengers Are Lost," November 19, 1906.

——. "Cause of the Dix Catastrophe," November 24, 1906.

AVALANCHE!
The Wellington Railway Disaster (1910)

Brady, J. P. "The Great Slide," *Railroad Magazine,* 1946.

Roe, J. *Stevens Pass: The Story of Railroading and Recreation in the North Cascades.* Caldwell, Idaho: Caxton Press, 2002.

Seattle Daily Times. "Avalanche Buries Train at Wellington," March 1, 1910.

——. "39 Dead, 27 Saved in Horror at Wellington," March 2, 1910.

——. "Avalanche at Wellington," March 3, 1910.

——. "Bodies May Not Be Recovered before Summer," March 3, 1910.

——. "Avalanche Costs Road Five Million Dollars," March 4, 1910.

———. "Key Men, Shut in by Big Slide, Near to Death," March 4, 1910.

———. "Coroner Brings Valuables of Slide Victims," March 5, 1910.

———. "Trainmaster Tells Story of Disaster," March 5, 1910.

———. "Bodies Brought to Seattle," March 7, 1910.

Tacoma Daily Tribune. "Believed Many Lives Lost in Catastrophe," March 1, 1910.

———. "Avalanche Horror Is Fully Confirmed in Official Advices," March 2, 1910.

———. "Awful Scenes Being Enacted at Wellington," March 3, 1910.

———. "Faint Hope That Wellington Missing May Be Alive," March 4, 1910.

———. "Baby Sat Cooing and Playing with the Snow," March 5, 1910.

———. "Graphic Story of Heartrending Scenes at Work," March 5, 1910.

———. "Wellington Is Shut off from Outside World," March 6, 1910.

Sherman, T. Gary. *Conquest and Catastrophe: The Triumph and Tragedy of the Great Northern Railway Through Stevens Pass.* Bloomington, Ind.: AuthorHouse, 2004.

"The Wellington Avalanche." USFS Web site: http://home1.gte.net/mvmmvm/index.html.

"Wellington Scrapbook—the 1910 Avalanche Disaster." HistoryLink Web site: www.historylink.org/wellington/overview.htm.

THE BIG BLOW
Western Washington Windstorm (1921)

"'The Great Blowdown' Windstorm Strikes to Washington Coast on January 29, 1921," HistoryLink Web site: www.historylink.org/essays/output.cfm?file_id=5249.

"Hurricane-Force Winds Kill 21 in Western Washington on October 21, 1934," HistoryLink Web site: www.historylink.org/essays/output.cfm?file_id=3734.

Morgan, M. *The Last Wilderness.* New York: Viking Press, 1955.

Read, W. "Olympic Blowdown of January 29, 1921," Storm King: Pacific Northwest Weather Events Web site: oregonstate.edu/~readw/January1921.html

———. "The Major Windstorm of October 21, 1934," Storm King: Pacific Northwest Weather Events Web site: oregonstate .edu/~readw/October1934.html.

"Some of the Area's Windstorms." National Weather Service—NWS Portland Web site: www.wrh.noaa.gov/pqr/paststorms/wind.php.

Tacoma News Tribune. "Storm-Battered Freighter Now in the Columbia," October 22, 1934.

MOCK BATTLE TURNS DEADLY
The Boeing Field Air Disaster (1937)

Seattle-Post Intelligencer. "Death Bares Romance and Broken Rule," November 4, 1937.

———. "How Death Came into Two Homes," November 4, 1937.

———. "Inquiry into Accident That Claimed 5 Opens Today," November 4, 1937.

———. "Witnesses Tell of Plane Crash," November 4, 1937.

———. "Versions Differ in Crash Probe," November 5, 1937.

Seattle Times. "Planes Hit over City; 5 Die!" November 3, 1937.

———. "Diving Ship Collapsed, Hit Bomber Says Pilot," November 4, 1937.

———. "Survivor in Air Disaster Describes Collision Cause to Coroner's Deputy; Naval Inquiry Board Named," November 4, 1937.

———. "Survivors of Crash Quizzed," November 5, 1937.

———. "Air Disaster Cause May Never Be Known," November 6, 1937.

GALLOPING GERTIE
The Tacoma Narrows Bridge Collapse (1940)

American Experience: Golden Gate Bridge. PBS, People & Events Web site: www.pbs.org/wgbh/amex/goldengate/peopleevents/p_moisseiff.html.

"'Galloping Gertie' Collapses November 7, 1940." Tacoma Narrows Bridge Connections, Washington State Department of Transportation Web site: www.wsdot.wa.gov/TNBhistory/Connections/connections3.htm.

"How and Why We Bridged the Narrows." Gig Harbor Peninsula Historical Society & Museum Web site: www.gigharbormuseum.org/nbonlinexhibit.html.

"Tacoma Narrows Bridge Collapses on November 7, 1940." HistoryLink Web site: www.historylink.org/essays/output.cfm?file_id=5048.

Tacoma News Tribune. "Cameraman Was on Cracking Span," November 8, 1940.

———. "Coatsworth First Thought of News," November 8, 1940.

———. "News Tribune Man Last on the Bridge," November 8, 1940.

———. "Span Mystery Man Had Big Thrill for Dime," November 9, 1940.

NOT HOME FOR THE HOLIDAYS
Mount Rainier Plane Crash (1946)

Arnold, Kenneth. "I Did See the Flying Disks," *Fate,* Spring 1948.

Barcott, Bruce. *The Measure of a Mountain: Beauty and Terror on Mount Rainier.* Seattle: Sasquatch Books, 1997.

"Enumclaw Veteran's Memorial Park—Marine Memorial." City of Enumclaw Web site: www.ci.enumclaw.wa.us/Photo _Tour_Marine.htm.

"In Memory of the Marines Lost on Mt. Rainier." Seattle Community Network Web site: www.scn.org/marines/ rainier.html.

Seattle Post-Intelligencer Reporter. "Ghosts of Mt. Rainier: A Majestic Tomb for 65 Men," March 29, 2000.

———. "Ghosts of Mt. Rainier: Glaciers, and Bodies Buried in Them, Are Slowly Sliding down the Mountain," March 29, 2000.

———. "Ghosts of Mt. Rainier: Profiles of the Missing," March 29, 2000.

———. "Ghosts of Mt. Rainier: God's Monument to 32 Marines," March 30, 2000.

Tacoma News Tribune, "Wreckage on Peak Sited," July 24, 1946.

———. "Three Parties Converge on Spot," July 25, 1946.

———. "Wreckage of Plane Identified," July 26, 1946.

———. "Search for Bodies on Glacier Given Up," July 28, 1946

———. "32 Aboard Wrecked Transport," December 12, 1946.

———. "Fear Lost Plane Over Glacier," December 13, 1946.

———. "Still Seek Plane on Glacier," December 13, 1946.

———. "Weather Aids Hunt for Plane," December 17, 1946.

———. "Hot Clue May Lead to Plane," December 18, 1946.

SHAKE, RATTLE, AND ROLL
The Puget Sound Earthquakes (1949 and 1965)

"Deep Quakes in Washington and Oregon." Pacific Northwest
    Seismic Network Web site: http://www.pnsn.org/INFO
    _GENERAL/platecontours.html.
"Earthquake Hits Puget Sound Area on April 13, 1949." HistoryLink
    Web site: historylink.org/essays/output.cfm?file_id=2063.
"Earthquake Rattles Western Washington on April 29, 1965."
    HistoryLink Web site: historylink.org/essays/output
    .cfm?file_id=1986.
Marvin Klegman Memorial Award, American Red Cross Mount
    Rainier Chapter Web site: www.rainier-redcross.org
    New_web/PROGRAMS/SPECIAL%20EVENTS/RHB/RHB%
    20Marvin%20Klegman%20Memorial%20Award.htm.
"State Honors Hero's Selfless Act." Northwest Cable News Web site:
    www.nwcn.com.
Tacoma News Tribune. "Tacoma Child Killed; Loss in Millions," April
    14, 1949.
———. "Geologist Says Slide Area Safe," April 17, 1949.
———. "Vast Slide Laid to Quake," April 18, 1949.

WASHINGTON'S HURRICANE
The Columbus Day Storm (1962)

Associated Press. "Murderous Storm Lashes State," October 13,
    2962.
"Columbus Day Storm—October 12, 1962." The *Columbian* Web
    site: www.columbian.com/history/Disasters/storm.cfm.
"More Great Memories—Columbus Day Storm 1962." The
    Columbian Web site: www.columbian.com/history/
    disasters/storm2page.cfm.

Seattle Times. "Very Dangerous Winds—New Storm Coming,"
     October 12, 1962.

————. "Gusts Attain 100 MPH—Storm at a Glance," October 13,
     1962.

"Some of the Area's Windstorms." National Weather Service—
     NWS Portland Web site: www.wrh.noaa.gov/pqr/paststorms/
     wind.php.

Tacoma News Tribune. "Storm Leaves Trail of Death, Destruction,"
     October 13, 1962.

THE BIG BLAST
The Mount St. Helens Eruption (1980)

"David A. Johnston: December 1949–May 18, 1980." USGS-
     Cascades Volcano Observatory Web site: vulcan.wr.usgs.gov/
     CVO_Info/david_johnston.html.

"Eruptions of Mt. St. Helens: Past, Present and Future." USGS—
     Cascades Volcano Observatory Web site: vulcan.wr.usgs.gov/
     Volcanoes/MSH/Publications/MSHPPF/MSH_past_present_
     future.html.

"Mt. St. Helens—May 18, 1980 Eruption Summary." USGS—
     Cascades Volcano Observatory Web site: vulcan.wr.usgs.gov/
     Volcanoes/MSH/May18/summary_may18_eruption.html.

News Tribune. "Five Stories Unfold under an Ashen Sky," May 18,
     2005.

Oregonian. "Survivors Recall Images of Eruption," May 15, 2000.

Seattle Post-Intelligencer, "In Seconds, a Mountain and Many Lives
     Were Lost." May 8, 2000.

Seattle Times. "Very Dangerous Winds—New Storm Coming."
     October 12, 1962.

FIRE FROM THE SKY
The Tyee Creek Fire (1994)

High Country News. "Fire and Blame in the Northwest: Loggers
    Urge Fire Sales," September 19, 1994.
News Tribune. "Runaway Blaze Rages in Dry Wind," July 26, 1994.
———. "Devastation Yields Scattered Miracles along Entiat River,"
    July 28, 1994.
Seattle Times. "Homes Threatened as Fire Rages On," July 26, 1994.
———. "Entiat Fire Beats Them All," July 28, 1994.
———. "Wildfire Sears 70,300 Acres; Residents Flee." July 29,
    1994.
———. "Fires Fuel Timber Industry Criticism of Clinton's Forest
    Plan," August 2, 1994.
"Tyee Creek Fire, 1994." HistoryLink Web site: www.historylink.org/
    cybertour/index.cfm?file_id=7061&frame=7.

A 6.8 SHAKER
The Nisqually Earthquake (2001)

"Earthquake Registering 6.8 on Richter Scale Jolts Seattle and
    Puget Sound on February 28, 2001." HistoryLink Web site:
    www.historylink.org/essays/output.cfm?file_id=3039.
"Northwest Earthquake." Official City of Olympia Web site:
    www.ci.olympia.wa.us/earthquake/default.asp.
News Tribune. "Quake Hits Home," March 1, 2001.
"Quake Leaves 17,000 without Power in U.S. Northwest," CNN
    Web site: archives.cnn.com/2001/US/02/28/northwest
    .quake.03/.
Seattle Times. "No Deaths, Few Serious Injuries in 6.8 Roller,"
    March 1, 2001.
———. "'The Tower Is Collapsing'—Sea-Tac Air Controllers Never
    Imagined They Would Be Landing Planes in an Earthquake.
    Now They're in a Trailer," March 3, 2001.

————. "Is Capitol Dome at Risk?" March 4, 2001.

————. "Why It's Called the Miracle Quake," March 4, 2001.

————. "Capitol Did Remarkably Well," March 5, 2001.

"Shaking, Liquefaction on Habor Island." Pacific Northwest Seismic Network Web site; www.ess.washington.edu/SEIS/EQ_Special/ WEBDIR_01022818543p/quakestory.html.

MEN, WOMEN, AND FIRE
The Thirtymile Fire (2001)

Seattle Times. "Training Is a Firefighter's Best Weapon," July 12, 2001.

————. "Survivor Recalls Deadly Afternoon," July 18, 2001.

"Thirtymile Fire, 2001." HistoryLink Web site: historylink.org/ cybertour/index.cfm?file_id=7061&frame=8.

USDA Forest Service. "Forest Service Chief Vows Changes from Thirtymile Fire," September 26, 2001.

Yakima Herald-Republic. "Deaths in Wildfire Avoidable, Inquiry Concludes," September 26, 2001.

About the Authors

NATALIE MCNAIR-HUFF has long been interested in the history of Washington state. She grew up in southwest Washington in Longview, where she was one of the many local residents living under the threat of flooding and more following the eruption of Mount St. Helens in 1980.

ROB MCNAIR-HUFF has also been a long-time history buff interested in Washington state's past. He grew up in Longview and then in Rochester, Washington, where he watched Mount St. Helens erupt from a distance.